The Productive Citizen

For Better Job . . .

Better Income . . .

Better World

Michael Sammaritano

Adesso Publishing Inc.

This publication is designed to provide accurate and authoritative information in regard to the subject matter covered. It is sold with the understanding that the publisher is not engaged in rendering legal, accounting, or other professional service. If legal advice or other expert assistance is required, the services of a competent professional person should be sought.

Library of Congress Cataloging-in-Publication Data
Michael Sammaritano
The Productive Citizen
Library of Congress Control Number 2010917555
ISBN 0-9779023-4-X
List Price $13.95 USA Dollars
Printed in the United States of America

10 9 8 7 6 5 4 3 2   Visit our website at
www.adessopublishing.com

To earn more money and simultaneously improve the economic well-being of his country, a worker has to be more productive to himself, to his job and to his family. This book reveals the basic skills to achieve that feat with ease.

*Throughout this book I refer to you, this worker, as **The Productive Citizen.** It includes wage-earners from all walks of life; professionals and non professionals alike. The world is in your hands. Individually we impact the world's prosperity.*

—Michael Sammaritano

Open Letter from the Author

Dear Reader,

After some fifty years of exploring the ups and downs of workers at large, let me assure you that every method presented in this book has passed the test of time, and is brought to you in a unique platform in which a successful career can be built without the hassle and frustrations others have experienced.

I have written this book as if I were a reporter hired by each and every worker who aspires to become a Productive Citizen. It is my intention to show you how to become a Productive Citizen and a high-wage-earner, to educate those the industries penalize for their lack of basic business skills, and to recruit the young people those same industries compete for into the rank of Productive Citizens.

For a fair assessment of your position in the world around you, you should ask: "Did I choose my career solely for a paycheck or for the challenges it offers?"

If your choice is based on both, challenge and a good paycheck, bear in mind that most success stories are the product of people's commitment to their cause and personal sacrifice.

The workplace has built many successful careers; it also has made many individuals too complacent to work themselves into the ranks of Productive Citizens.

From my personal experience, I have concluded that what makes these individuals complacent, or, should I say, fearful of taking the next step is lack of basic business and commonsense skills, and therefore the confidence to overcome the obstacles each challenge presents.

You might ask "What do business or commonsense skills have to do with a worker who works for a living?" and I would say it is the difference between success and failure in your career. Stay the course and the answer will become apparent later on in this book.

Confidence, knowledge, and commitment are words that rarely amount to anything without the willingness to sacrifice. Of all the successful methods I have studied one stands out as supreme—the willingness to sacrifice for the sake of nourishing a rewarding career and a prosperous country—your country, as opposed to that of the fellow who just seeks wages without sacrifice.

The sacrifice I refer to does not mean restraining your lifestyle to a poverty level. It simply means using your learning resources—time and money—judiciously.

In essence, if you want the kind of success you've seen others achieve, you must embrace commitment and sacrifice as part of your mission. Most of the methods presented in this book are meant to alleviate your degree of sacrifice but not your degree of commitment. In fact, you should intensify your commitment with each successful step you take. For example, have the commitment to learn as much as you can so you might contribute something of value to your job which, in turn, will pay you back many times over.

In life we rarely find those willing to tell us how things are done. And if and when we do, or if we discover the answers ourselves, it usually happens when we've lost the zeal to apply this newfound knowledge.

Best of luck,

—Michael Sammaritano

TABLE OF CONTENTS

Chapter 1

THE PRODUCTIVE CITIZEN DEFINED

THE PRODUCTIVE CITIZEN

For the purposes of this work, a Productive Citizen is a member of the workforce of any democratic country. He controls productivity which is directly related to inflation—the root of prosperity.

The Productive Citizen, besides being a good standing citizen, must possess basic business skills for his trade or profession, which can help promote him and his employer to the people of the industry they serve.

The status of Productive Citizen should not be confused with nor determined by the amount of work he puts out in any given hour for that has nothing to do with the productive status one earns as a valued member of a managerial team.

In that capacity, your productivity ratio is no longer measured by physical work output but by the effect your actions and decisions have on the company's bottom line. Therefore dedication, enthusiasm, and loyalty are your best tools.

THE JOB

The integrity of a Productive Citizen will not allow him to impose himself on a job; he will always earn his position.

In a workplace, you earn the position you're competing for by creating demand for your skills and personality. As a pro, you will always live up to, or exceed, your own expectations. When you make difficult performances look easy, people will cheer you the same way they cheer athletes. You'll hold the arena.

Along the way, you'll find that the best competitive edges are your positive attitude, your desire to learn, and your courage to apply the knowledge you possess in all you do. Developing this trio and taking them to higher levels will always create higher standards for your overall performance and build you a successful career supported by those for whom you work.

For those who are new to this principle, be assured that it applies to all who are seeking a better job—beginners and veterans alike. Perhaps the following analogy on inflation and supply and demand will shed some light on the subject.

Inflation, to most people, is the difference between cost and value. If you pay a dollar for a service that is only worth seventy cents, then you lose thirty cents for every dollar you spend on that service—a thirty percent inflation, if you will. Conversely, if you pay a dollar for something that is worth one dollar and thirty cents, then your dollar has deflated by thirty percent—a thirty-cent gain in your dollar value. All things being equal, the latter will always translate into high demand and short supply assuring job security and financial success to all who help maintain that ratio.

This principle is mainly responsible for healthy relationships between employees and employers, and the financial success or failure of individuals, companies, and nations. Even though inflation's inner workings are more complex—for there are many other contributing factors—productivity is the most important. Your degree of productivity will either increase or decrease the value of every dollar circulated—and most often affect the stability of the very job you hold.

Regardless of reasons or outcome, when we honestly produce to the best of our abilities, we've reached peak performance. We can average that performance into national statistics or we can individualize it by just concerning ourselves with our own circumstance.

In doing so, we can either be content and accept the results, or try to be more productive and seek ways and means to improve the value of our performance.

Individually, we can get to the core of the matter and conclude that no other formula than supply and demand can be more to our advantage. It rewards those who are willing to improve and penalizes those who are complacent and skeptical.

However, creating demand can be complex at times— especially when we cannot freely dedicate ourselves to that cause. Past experiences, greed, prejudices and the like can interfere with our pride and natural desire to excel. Others' opinions can also inhibit our potential, thus affecting performance. For example, the traditional grandfathering of a job because someone in the family is a longtime employee of a company most often leads to complacency—an attitude responsible for massive layoffs.

A productive person must always pay attention to these factors. If not, he can easily get caught on the downswing and become a liability rather than a productive team member. This undoubtedly is a position you don't want to get caught in, for it will force you into imposing yourself on your job, rather than earning your position; thus decreasing self-esteem and job security substantially.

A productive person's job security lies in his ability to market his skills as a businessperson markets his products or services. As a free agent, he can contract himself for short or long periods with no fear of running out of work. For as long as he keeps himself updated on the latest methods and technology, throughout his career he may work for several employers. In fact, to stay in tune with the times, we may say he can schedule his career calendar as freelancer servicing several contracts.

As an employee, you are selling your talent to the company you work for every day. Thoughts such as "I'm making my boss rich," "Why should I produce more" or "The more I work, the less I get paid for" have no place in your formula for success. You are obliged to yourself and to your self-esteem to always be the best you can be in all you do. If you're productive and dedicated to the job, you can rest assured you will have a secure career with an income well above average.

Improving your overall performance and recognizing your potential can easily put you on top of the heap, creating high demand for your talent, which is your most precious asset. Your boss will recognize the increase in your value as a productive worker long before you do. For it is in his best interest to spot and retain good productive people.

THE AVERAGE WORKER

The average worker is a person who does, as the title implies, an average days' work. In addition, this worker is also a person with feelings and dreams of his own.

If such a worker wants to excel beyond the point of just

being a worker into a managerial position such as lead person, foreman, manager or general manager, then he must expand his skills beyond workmanship to achieve his goal successfully. He must be proficient in the business side of his field of expertise. He must also know how to deal with customers, manage employees, and get along with co-workers.

Typically, a worker, as he comes up through the ranks, will learn all about the rules and regulations of good safety and workmanship in his industry. In contrast, he will not be taught basic business skills—which are essential to enter the managerial position as a productive worker.

Besides expected to be a master of his trade or profession, a worker, without formal training, is most often expected to represent his employer as if he were a seasoned businessperson capable of selling, making business decisions, and executing complex contract documents. While this is ludicrous, unfortunately, it is very true in many small businesses.

Most workers, due to their continuing exposure to intricate work, develop a logical mind capable of interpreting and deciphering complex documents.

Without any conscious effort on their part, this comes about by the time they rise to the level of accomplished worker.

If you have the desire to become a productive worker, you must keep your dreams alive and declare yourself at the one-yard line of your aspiring career.

In this book, progressively and systematically, you will learn about marketing, contract interpretation and its relationship to the contract, proposal contracts, dealing with customers, and many other aspects the job may call for.

Your representations and decisions will be logical and sound. Your newfound knowledge will give you the confidence to always be in control of your job and will keep you in high demand.

THE PRODUCTIVE WORKER'S JOB

As a productive worker you must be able to switch jobs on demand. You may be needed as a serviceman on one occasion or as a foreman or even manager on another. Regardless of which position you're called to do, be aware that everything you do or say is binding to the company you work for—your employer. At these times, you are the company.

The successful outcome of the business relationship between your employer and the customer is entirely up to you. Your attitude and your business and technical skills are direct reflections of yourself and of your employer.

In fact, more often than not, what attracts people to a company is one or more personal traits of the people who represent the company—you, rather than the company itself. People deal with people, not with objects or abstractions.

In short, the reason a productive worker will always be in high demand is because he can easily fulfill these requirements successfully and productively—a win-win situation for the employer and the employee.

FINDING YOUR POSITION

Throughout your waking hours—whether or not you work for others and whether you want it or not—you are always marketing yourself and the company you work for.

The effectiveness of your promotion is the result of this subconscious effort. Depending on your general attitude, your knowledge of the subject at hand and the enthusiasm you display, your marketing effort will always have either a positive or a negative result. The latter is self-destructive and undoubtedly responsible for failures. It will always hold you back like a large lead ball chained to your ankle.

If you happen to be on the winning side of that equation, that's good. On the other hand, if you happen to be on the losing side and want to excel or if you wonder why you're constantly coming across stumbling blocks, then you should take a good inventory of yourself. Make a conscientious effort to improve in those problem areas that show up in the following two assessment tables.

At this crossroads, these two tables will guide you through an important challenge—finding out how you stand in you industry's marketplace and understanding the effect your personal traits, business skills, and technical skills have on your career and earning power.

Personal Assessment Table

Code: R = Required/ beneficial to you P = Possess it now (8-10 M = Must Improve (1-7)		Self-rating. Use a 1 to 10 scale, 1 being low, 10 high		Productive Lead person			Productive Foreman			Productive Manager			Productive General Manager		
		Before	After	R	P	M	R	P	M	R	P	M	R	P	M
	PERSONAL TRAITS														
1.	Appearance			✓			✓			✓			✓		
2.	Punctuality			✓			✓			✓			✓		
3.	Enthusiasm			✓			✓			✓			✓		
4.	Assertiveness			✓			✓			✓			✓		
5.	Communication			✓			✓			✓			✓		
6.	Reliability			✓			✓			✓			✓		
7.	Foresight			✓			✓			✓			✓		
8.	Following Instructions			✓			✓			✓			✓		
	Personal Score:														
	BUSINESS SKILLS														
1.	Time Management			✓			✓			✓			✓		
2.	Motivating Leadership			✓			✓			✓			✓		
3.	Decision-Making			✓			✓			✓			✓		
4.	Organizational Skills			✓			✓			✓			✓		
5.	Planning			✓			✓			✓			✓		
6.	Marketing			✓			✓			✓			✓		
7.	Purchasing			✓			✓			✓			✓		
8.	Recordkeeping			✓			✓			✓			✓		
	Business Score:														
	TECHNICAL SKILLS														
1.	Trade Code knowledge			✓			✓			✓			✓		
2.	Install and repair work			✓			✓			✓			✓		
3.	Plans and specs reading			✓			✓			✓			✓		
4.	Decipher schematics			✓			✓			✓			✓		
5.	Basic calculus			✓			✓			✓			✓		
6.	Layout work			✓			✓			✓			✓		
7.	Knowledge of other trades			✓			✓			✓			✓		
8.	Safety regulations			✓			✓			✓			✓		
	Technical Skills Score:														
	Total Score:														

Through the "Personal Assessment Table," you can rate yourself before and after you embark on your journey. Before you use this table, make a photocopy so you can use it later on for further evaluations. Or, instead of rating yourself, you may consult the opinion of someone you trust. Use the "Before" and "After" columns for this purpose and date both events. As your score goes up, so will your value as a productive worker.

You will notice that the right side of the form is divided into five columns; each headed by the word 'Productive,' followed by a job classification such as Lead Person, Foreman, Manager, and General Manager. Each classification column is subdivided into three smaller columns: R, P, and M.

Each imprinted check-mark in the R column indicates that the subject is either 'Required' or very beneficial for the productive fulfillment of that job classification.

For example, to qualify as a Productive Lead Person, as defined in this book, you must possess a score at or above the guidelines set for each skill or personal trait check-marked in the R column under the Productive

Lead Person heading. This process is then repeated for the Foreman, Manager and General Manager.

The 'P' (Possess it now) column, can only be checked off if your self-rating for a specific subject is between 8 and 10. Any score less than 8 will force you to check-mark the 'M' (Must improve) column.

On this principle, as you improve in your weaker areas you will find yourself progressing toward becoming an accomplished productive worker capable of holding any of the four jobs listed at will.

Your personal traits score should not be less than 70.

Your business skills score should not be less than 65.

Your technical skills score should not be less than 65.

To be at the top of the heap, your combined score should total no less than 200, at which level you can congratulate yourself on being an accomplished worker who will always be in high demand.

Job Description and Qualification Table

Code: R = Required/ beneficial to you P = Possess it now M = Must Improve Job Requirements	Subject Reference Chptr	Productive Lead Person			Productive Foreman			Productive Manager			Productive General Manager		
		R	P	M	R	P	M	R	P	M	R	P	M
1 Market yourself and the company	1, 2	✓			✓			✓			✓		
2 Deal with the customer	2	✓			✓			✓			✓		
3 Prepare for and attend meetings	2				✓			✓			✓		
4 Contract basics	6	✓			✓			✓			✓		
5 Prepare/execute: Proposal/Contract	6										✓		
6 Contracts and negotiation	7										✓		
7 Protect the contracted work	8	✓			✓			✓			✓		
8 Maintain progress schedules	2							✓			✓		
9 Collections	9										✓		
10 Work compliance	2, 8	✓			✓			✓			✓		
Total Classification Credits:		5			6			7			10		

This table gives you an overview of the four job classifications. Each requirement attained is given a value of one credit. Through this chart you can determine what the industry expects from each classification, how well you qualify, and, all things being equal, what you're worth when compared to your local average pay-rate—should you ask for a pay raise or demote yourself? Or better yet, should you get to work on improving your present position?

The totals of each 'R' column represent the number of credits 'Required' to qualify for each job classification. Equate one of these totals to your local average pay for that classification and you will determine a credit pay-value. Multiply this value by the number of credits required in each of the remaining classifications and you'll find the average pay-scale for each classification.

For example, if a Lead person's average pay, in your area, is $18.50 per hour, you can determine that each credit-value is $3.70 ($18.50 divided by column 'R' 5 credits equals $3.70). Therefore, with each class being in direct relationship to the same level of expertise and the number of job assignments, we can further determine a basic pay scale for each of them.

In the first case the $3.70 credit-value should earn an hourly rate of $22.20 for the Foreman's 6 credits; $25.90 for the manager's 7 credits; and $37.00 for the General Manager's 10 credits.

This equation is obviously based on full qualification of the minimum requirements shown in the table. For example, the Lead person whose rate is used for our equation must fully qualify on all 5 credits.

If the assessment table reveals that you are holding a

position with less credits than those required, then you should multiply this lower number by the same credit-value to find your true hourly-rate worth. If you're paid more than you're worth, then your job is in jeopardy—not to mention the negative effect your lack of knowledge has on the company's bottom line.

Painful as it might be, be honest with yourself and do something about it because the security of your job or the future of your company is in jeopardy. In essence, the message is clear: If you want job security and average or above-average pay, you must earn your position and not impose it.

To help you in this endeavor, the 'Subject Reference' column indicates the Chapter in this book where you can study a specific subject in depth. If need be, you may consider additional study outside the realm of this book that may help you with work habits and general attitude.

This table offers you the unique opportunity to evaluate yourself in depth and to target those areas needing improvement. When you have followed these guidelines and progressed to your ultimate goal, then be confident that your newly earned position is secured by the most powerful tool known to man—knowledge, qualifying you as a Productive Citizen for you are contributing something of values to your country's economy—productivity.

WHAT'S AHEAD

If we recognize that the successful growth of a company is ultimately dependent on the knowledge of its managerial team and its ability to focus harmoniously on the same objectives, then we can also recognize that the ultimate knowledge of the team members must be in synch with each other and with the company's ultimate objectives.

For example, your employer's resources, knowledge, and business skills will be far more effective if all the members of his managerial team worked by the same business principles he does; rather than an array of methods based on bits and pieces of business skills acquired by trial and error and most often experienced by one member only.

The most productive way to develop a harmonious team capable of focusing collectively and individually on the company's objectives is for all members of that team, including the owner, to adopt business methods of which each member is knowledgeable or has an opportunity to learn. Those methods must be all taken from the same source.

To carry out the feat of bringing forth personal and business skills to this learning platform for the array of trades and professions, I have chosen the business operating manual of electrical contracting. The personal and business skills required by this industry are well in synch and oftentimes above most other industries. Therefore, the following chapters are an adaptation of my book *Electrical Contracting,* first published in 2001.

While some subjects may seem out of the realm of the work at hand, you should pay particular attention to these extraordinary subjects, for they will help you understand your industry's business better. The material ahead is relevant to the discovery of your relative position in your industry as well as to your general development as a Productive Citizen.

Someday you may be called on to take over your boss's job and you won't want to miss that opportunity for lack of this basic knowledge. As stated in the beginning, this book offers you the unique opportunity to be the best you can be in your industry.

What's ahead in this manual is a combination of educational subjects relevant to the previous two tables and to your general development as a productive worker. Some chapters will delve into the job of your employer in order to acquaint you with some of the problems he has to deal with to run a successful operation.

Chapter 2

MARKET YOURSELF . . .

THIS AND OTHER CHAPTERS

This chapter deals with marketing yourself and the company you work for to the customer with whom you come in contact, whether directly or indirectly. The first requisite of a productive worker is to promote yourself and your company to the industry you serve. This kind of loyalty is an unwritten rule that applies to all employees.

While several references in this and other chapters in this book can easily apply to the way you market yourself to your employer, their basic purpose is to teach fundamental business skills that will help you become a valuable member of your company's managerial team.

If you need to review how to market yourself to your employer go back to the introduction *Open Letter* and *Chapter 1.*

MARKET YOURSELF

Historically, illegal and unqualified businesses have often enticed prospective customers with the lure of low prices, setting a trend that greatly affects the legitimate business. Shady marketers with slick presentations quite often take away business from qualified businesses that have yet to learn the art of effective marketing.

As a serious business' representative, you must recognize and deal with this trend, as well as with other competitive elements. You must follow or help generate a comprehensive marketing plan that allows you to market yourself and the company; not only to prospective customers, but to the whole industry.

Those who underestimate the value of a marketing strategy usually leave behind a trail of misleading impressions that foster endless negative repercussions, affecting the company they work for and all they do.

FIRST IMPRESSIONS

When you promote yourself, either by personal contact or by printed matter, it is important to leave behind a favorable impression. The visual impact you create, followed by your spoken words, are judged and forever recorded in people's minds. That impression is also labeled with their perception of who you led them to believe you are and what you led them to believe you do. This label is usually a product of your presentation, and, once set in their minds, it rarely changes. First impressions are inerasable and unchangeable. From that moment on, every subsequent contact you make with them will trigger their first impression of you.

If a person first presents himself as a serviceperson to a customer and later on wants to change his image to that of a businessperson, for example, he can never upgrade his rank in his customer's mind-eye unless he first presents himself as a well-rounded businessperson, even when performing service work. The image he creates first is how that customer will label him no matter how hard he tries to change later on.

Regardless of the rank you choose—serviceperson, lead person, foreman, manager, general manager, or whatever else you may choose—you should never make careless or un-businesslike presentations. Unprofessional presentations create long-lasting damage to your image, and lead prospective customers to either look elsewhere for a better company, or to treat your company as shady and unworthy of their business, unless their risk is well compensated. When the latter takes place, suddenly your lowest price is not low enough, no matter how hard you try to make the sale.

But favorable impressions serve only as door openers to better opportunities. They are not signed contracts. They are to be treated no differently than telephone calls generated by solicitations. What happens with these opportunities is entirely up to you and your ability to sell and close contracts. Once you take a job, the quality of your company's performance will then complement your other virtues. This determines the type of relationship you establish between your company and the customers. Will they call you back?

FIRST MEETINGS

In making sales presentations, be aware that the first question in prospective customers' mind is: "Who are you? Who's your company?" And unless you're ready to answer promptly and satisfy this and other pertinent questions, the presentation can easily turn into a very uncomfortable and non-productive meeting.

In a well-planned marketing approach, your promotional material has to lead up to your personal presentation. This approach will familiarize the prospective customer with you and your company and pave the way for productive sales calls. When you finally meet your prospective customer, there will be no question as to who you are or who your company is. The sale will then be the meeting's focal point.

However, when the occasion arises that you have to make "cold calls" in person, one sure way to avoid embarrassment and win the prospective customer's confidence is to be ready to answer all questions and to overcome the "Who are you?" question within the first few seconds of the meeting. This is done, not by magic, but by an efficient presentation adhering to some basic guidelines. For a productive worker, the things-to-do list is simple and concise:

Personal Appearance

Most people observe people from their feet up. Good clean shoes, neatly groomed hair and complementary attire will do the job.

Show yourself to be ready to do business by carrying a briefcase or a well-organized notebook.

GENERAL ATTITUDE

- Be positive and enthusiastic about the topic at hand. Show your expertise and genuine interest in the project.
- Pay close attention to what your prospective customer is saying.
- Express your opinions freely.
- Do not use his telephone for any other purposes than your presentation. When you have to, be very discreet.
- Converse with your prospective customer.
- Humor, when out of place, can be costly. Jokes and other trivial conversation should be left for the water-cooler breaks.

- Do not hide your traits; they are your assets and you should appropriately promote them.

- Do not throw ice cubes on a warming-up relationship. In other words, do not use phrases such as "Yes, Sir" or "Yes, Ma'am" or the like. There is nothing wrong with addressing customers by their names. When someone is warming up to you, it is because he begins to trust you and wants to get closer. A too formal conversation can distance your prospective customer to an irretrievable corner. Seize the moment, and share his enthusiasm in the most cordial and friendly way. If he warms up to you, respond in the same way. Your prospective customer, before he signs the contract, wants and needs to feel comfortable with you and your company.

- Do not make constant reference to the National Code. Use your mechanic's expert opinion. Remember any Code requirements are minimum standards of good workmanship. Most projects are designed and built above minimum standards.

- No snow jobs: You are better off saying nothing than faking a compliment.

- Also remember that telling someone you or your company is licensed adds little value to your presentation. You are expected to be licensed. On the other hand, to tell someone you do work above industry standards adds considerable value to your presentation.

MARKET YOUR COMPANY

Before we start on the subject of marketing your company, we need to address a misconception that concerns many industries. The primary intent behind marketing a company (not to be confused with marketing a company's product or service) is to enhance and present the company as a whole to prospective customers.

Misleading promotional campaigns are the main cause of many consumer losses with costly backlashes to the promoting company itself. For example, a growing company that is working hard at creating demand for its services makes unjustified changes to their marketing plans in midstream. Many executives consider natural growth to be too slow. When that happens, they begin to doubt sound marketing approaches, they disregard their company's ability to produce and, at the flip of a coin, embark on a new and more aggressive campaign, thus generating more sales than the company can handle. This misleading campaign adversely affects the customer and the company as well, especially when orders are mishandled.

We need not be seasoned marketers to spot the problems facing these companies. They simply are not set up to handle overnight growth; for that matter, very few companies are. The additional workload can easily put them out of business.

Marketing plans have to be laid out with care. Their implementation must be executed with greater care. And their results need to be patiently nurtured for long-term growth.

Promoting a company for a job for which it is undercapitalized or not equipped to handle, will burden the company's natural growth. Natural business growth is achieved by letting the business grow at its own pace and on its own merit. This means the company should undertake only profitable jobs that it can handle with ease. Consistent profit-making gives confidence in a marketing plan, which in turn nurtures good organization—an essential element in the natural growth of long-term plans.

Forced business growth, on the other hand, besides being a gamble, will lead to disorganized plans, with daily tasks being run on emergency bases, and new personnel training reduced to almost nothing. When a company puts itself in that position, it will soon find itself having neither the resources nor the organization to complete the work.

To prevent such a situation, once a company has reached its workload capacity, it has to turn down a customer or a seemingly profitable job no matter how hard this may be. The company can't take on additional work just on gut feeling. Decisions must be based on facts and figures and a good plan to expand its work capability. Some may think this rule applies only to manufacturers or larger contractors. This could not be further from the truth. It applies more to the beginner than it does to large established companies.

As wise and successful businesspersons, the principals of the company must update themselves on its financial status and production capabilities on a daily basis. This knowledge will give them the confidence to make wise decisions. With it, they may take calculated risks and undertake additional work, or they can build the courage to turn down jobs that, in their opinion, regardless of anticipated profits, are a sure liability to the company.

If you worry about the company losing customers by turning down work, don't worry. In such cases, the first thing the company has to consider is its responsibility toward its employees and itself. In these situations, the company may turn its predicament into a powerful marketing tool. Explaining to your customers why you are turning down their work will only strengthen your business ties. Everyone wants a winner. You will be planting a very good seed for the future, thus creating greater demand for your company. This customer will not only call on your company early for his next project, but will influence others to call on you as well by talking about your integrity and the successful operation of your company.

Good, effective marketing plans grow at their own pace. After all, the seeds you plant for your company are the seeds for your personal future as well. Because so much depends on them, when we sense a delay or decline in sales, it is a common syndrome among planners and executives to start doubting the very plan they created and implemented. These are moments in life, however, when a company has to believe in its managerial team and patiently stay put.

This is not to imply that marketing plans are written in stone. If a company feels it has given its marketing plan a reasonable chance to work, by all means it should make adjustments as it goes along. But it should be done prudently, because neither you nor anyone else in the company can predict where, when or how many seeds are about to germinate. A company should make changes, but never stray from good marketing fundamentals.

A COMPANY MARKETING PLAN

For a company, implementing an effective, comprehensive marketing plan usually does not add to its advertising costs. At times it even cuts its budget. Chances are it's paying for some form of advertising— for example, stationery, truck lettering, specialty items, yellow pages and the like. Most often, the only thing the company needs to do is to rework and synchronize them with those missing elements that are needed to achieve its objectives.

A common alternative to a comprehensive marketing plan is a random plan. As the title implies, it's a combination of traditional marketing elements, most often copied from others, and the adoption of randomly selected, ineffective bits and pieces of advertising and specialty items.

At times, such plans may give the appearance of a comprehensive marketing plan. Ironically, though, with a strong compulsion to invest in advertising on one hand, and cut expenses on the other, a company's owner creates costly and ineffective marketing plans, thus squandering good promotional dollars.

To convert ineffective advertising items into effective elements for a new comprehensive marketing plan, a company should begin, for example, with the truck lettering. Next time it's lettering a truck, it should make sure the overall layout sends the message it wants. Next, it should do the same with its stationery and so on. (How to do this is detailed later in this chapter.)

In comparing cost versus effectiveness of individual marketing elements, a company will find, amazingly, that the least expensive are the most effective. A well-written company reference letter, for example, or the implementation of standard procedures aimed at the enhancement of the company's overall performance, are the most common among these items.

Starting out in business, most company owners pay little or no attention to image setting and visual impact. In many instances it is the last thing on most people's minds. However, for the someday-to-be-successful-company, starting up is the best time to follow the owner's visions and plan where it wants to be five, ten or twenty years down the road.

For those who are committed to going the full mile, the implementation of a marketing plan is a serious matter and as such should not be left in the hands of others. Copywriters and commercial artists can only create from what a company's owner or manager shows and tells them. If the owner wants his experience and wisdom reflected in his work, then, contrary to what he thought or to what he's accustomed to, he must provide them with specific guidelines as well as his visions.

Following is a list of the major marketing elements pertaining to contracting or any other form of business. The commentary notes are designed to acquaint the company's owner or manager with acceptable guidelines for creating effective marketing campaigns. An owner should be directly involved in the future of his company. He should study these notes in detail, for they will give him, and you, the basic knowledge to define effective marketing plans. Learning these elements will help you in your endeavor to become a Productive Citizen.

VISUAL IMPACT

Logo

A logo is the catalyst of the company. It is the image setter that tells what the company is, what it does, and it must portray the same message regardless of its size and color. While it should be unique, it does not have to be clever. The best design for a logo is simple in color and layout. A logo, due to its different applications will sometimes be reduced to a very small size, or enlarged greatly. It will also be photocopied in black and white, especially in today's world of facsimile (fax) machines. If it's loaded with many or tiny details, and too many shades of color, those details will be lost when the logo is reduced or be out of proportion when it's enlarged. The most effective are graphic logos.

Truck Lettering

The best and most inexpensive mobile advertising space is the free space on a truck's outside panels. A contractor must use all sides of that truck, including the top when necessary. But as often as their trucks are seen on the road, many company waste this valuable advertising space. For example, a majority of them rarely use the rear or the front panel and never the top.

Using the top of a service truck is very effective advertising, especially when serving business and residential communities with two-story buildings and larger. When a truck is parked between other vehicles, the top panel has a greater audience than the side panels. The people on the ground level are usually in a hurry, while the people up above; attracted by the novelty, have the time to write down the company's name and phone number. If a contractor decides to use the top panel of his trucks and must also place the ladders up there, then share the space between the ladders and the sign. He must move and stack the ladders to the side opposite the sign.

Lettering the rear of the truck, because of the long-time exposure it has for those who follow your truck, can't be neglected. Too many companies, to save a few dollars when ordering lettering, are wasting this valuable space.

The general guidelines for truck lettering are as important as the location of the lettering on your truck.

Do not clutter the lettering with too much text. Every word used, in its proper place and size, has to say something of value (No ego trips here).

The size of each line should be consistent and proper. The name of the company should be 100%, the telephone number 75%, a slogan 30%, and the rest of the text, if any, should be proportionally smaller.

License Numbers and The Like

License numbers, though they are required and though they reassure the public of the company legitimacy, they don't carry much advertising weight; no matter how large the letters are. They should be treated as normal text, 30% or less of the company's name.

Telephone Numbers

Whenever possible, a contractor should avoid the use of multiple telephone numbers—for example, one for each location he works in. This type of listing tends to clutter the truck lettering, and takes the reader's attention from the message. If the intent is to make it convenient for anyone to call the company from remote locations, then adopt a toll-free number. The toll-free number also serves to overcome people's reluctance to call out-of-town contractors. It's a good business rule to pay for business calls generated by the company advertising. In business, a contractor will always pay for leads one way or another.

Color and Font Typefaces

The use of too many colors should not be employed; the maximum should be three colors. The same applies to font and typeface styles for the letters.

Company Logo

A well-displayed company logo on a truck or sign will pull more than any logo printed on business cards and letterheads put together. This is because the truck or sign is exposed to larger audiences for greater periods of time than a business card or letterhead, which are usually seen only by those that are personally solicited or the company deals with. This is only a comparison between outdoor signs and general stationery, and not a recommendation to remove the logo from the company stationery. The logo is important in that it delivers the impact for all the company's visual marketing tools. The comparison here is made to encourage the placement of the logo on trucks and signs, a neglected item by many contractors.

Therefore, next time a contractor wants to cut the truck lettering costs, he should shop for better prices rather than omit the logo. Besides, there are most likely many other items from the truck lettering layout that are ineffective and a contractor can delete, not only bringing his cost down, but also improving the overall impact of the company's message.

Paint or Vinyl Lettering

For all his sign needs, whenever possible, a contractor should use cut-to-specifications vinyl letters instead of hand-painted lettering. The vinyl lettering lasts longer, better resists the effects of weather, and does not discolor as fast as painted letters do. The overall look is also superior.

If budget is his problem, many vinyl lettering suppliers will cut his letters and logo to his specifications. With a little guidance from them, he can install it himself and save enough on labor to afford lettering for all five sides of the truck plus the company's logo.

Job Site Signs

The same rules that apply to truck lettering basically apply to any form of sign lettering with few exceptions:

- Unlike truck signs, job site signs are fixed, and passing traffic must get their message at a glance, thus limiting the text a contractor can place on them. The logo and company's name should be the most prominent elements. Job site signs, when well proportioned in line size, font, and color, pull a good share of advertising load. Because they are placed near a job that a company is doing, they act as testimonial to its success and are therefore very effective. Placing one sign at each job site around town will give the company the best credentials it can have.

- A contractor should avoid popular layout signs where *"Another Job By"* or *"Electrical Work By"* lines are larger than the company's name. If the sign is next to a construction site, it's obvious that the company is doing that job. To add any other line will obscure the company name and logo.

- A contractor should keep the same lettering proportions for his sign lettering that he used on the truck: name and logo 100%, telephone number 75%, all other lines 30% or smaller. He should check that every word says something of value. He should not clutter the sign with unnecessary words or lines and he should make use of good contrasting colors.

Uniforms

Uniforms are a necessity for service-oriented companies. Their color scheme and lettering should stay in harmony with the rest of the company's attire. A contractor should use identification tags for each serviceperson instead of imprinting their names on the uniform.

Identification tags

Identification tags add prestige to the company. The customer feels the company has taken the time, which a contractor should, to individually check and identify its employees, especially when the employee photo is included. Identification tags make it easy for exchanging uniforms and are a requirement in most security-sensitive areas. Many times, the mention in a marketing reference letter of the company using uniforms and identification tags for its servicemen is the difference between losing and getting a job or a maintenance contract.

Hard Hats

Hard hats are good safety devices. OSHA requires them on all job sites. From a marketing point of view, they are very effective. The next time you see a cover page featuring a contractor at work, note the two main elements of visual impact. Both a hard hat and a company's name and logo enhance the publication's feature story, as well as the subject contractor. Visualize the same photos without hard hats and you will understand the power of visual impact.

Indisputably, hard hats make a statement about the company. Those who think it's inconvenient or unimportant to make their employees wear hard hats should consider safety as well as marketing advantages. The use of hard hats makes good business sense since, for relatively little cost, it creates a safer work environment with fewer accidents and lower insurance premiums while giving the company greater visibility.

COMMUNICATION

Stationery

A letter is the physical messenger of your thoughts to whomever you want to address them. Its appearance dictates the impression you will create on the reader.

Many volumes have been written on business letter-writing content, text formats, and layout including crafted letters for any business occasion. If you need help in business letter writing, you are encouraged to follow the guidelines as laid out in specially crafted business letters. They are an excellent learning tool.

There are certain conventions used in letter writing that are well established, yet they are flexible enough to allow us to communicate exactly what we want to our reader. If we consider the appearance of a company letter, including the stationery, format, length, and envelope, the reader will be drawn to it. Once the reader gives a letter his or her attention, your message is sure to get through.

The Envelope

The appearance of the envelope adds to the overall professional appearance of the company letter. With the exception of using the two-letter abbreviation for the state, the address on the envelope should appear exactly the same as the inside address of the letter.

The Letterhead

The letterhead usually consists of the company logo, the company full business name and address, license number, phone and facsimile (fax) number. The information included should be uncluttered and readable. The design should be simple enough for the reader to find the information he or she needs without being distracted from reading the rest of the letter.

The fax number is an additional (electronic) mailing address and as such, it belongs with the address, possibly on the same line and right after the zip code. Contrary to conventional practices, it does not belong next to the telephone number. The telephone number clearly belongs by itself, clear of clutter.

Business stationery usually is white or some other conservative color. The standard size of the stationery is 8.5 by 11 inches.

The letterhead is always used only for the first sheet of a letter. If the typed letter is more than one page, a plain sheet of paper matching the letterhead should be used for subsequent pages.

The length of any letter affects its appearance. Customers who receive a lot of correspondence every day are not going to react favorably to lengthy three-page letters that could have been written in one page.

Come right to the point in your letters. They should be concise and limited to one page if possible.

PRINTED AD

The general guidelines for effective visual impact that a company owner has learned here also applies to printed ads in publications, telephone directories, circulars, brochures and specialty items. These guidelines, combined with his marketing objectives, will help him create the most effective layout for his next printed advertise.

PERFORMANCE

As a promotional tool, nothing has a more lasting marketing effect than good company performance. The quality of its performance perhaps will not generate a great deal more business at first, but a contractor can be certain that in time it will become his company's hallmark.

To gain such a reputation takes a conscientious and collective effort by every member of the company. A company should adopt policies that will deliver quality products or service with integrity, then it will be on its way to an unstoppable success. The following topics pertain to this subject:

Punctuality

The worst feeling you can have is to walk into a meeting and instead of saying *"Good morning,"* or *"Good afternoon,"* you have to say *"I am sorry I'm late,"* or make up excuses for being late. The worst part is not your feelings being hurt, but your reputation as a responsible individual and that of the company you work for being seriously damaged. Frequent incidents like these adversely influence decision-makers.

If you are a habitually tardy person and wish to experience what others experience when you are late, just think back to a situation when someone was late for an appointment with you. As the time approached, you began to check your wristwatch. At about five minutes before the hour, you began to formulate doubtful thoughts about that person. At the top of the hour your doubtful thoughts changed to unprintable language that got progressively worse with every passing minute. Fifteen minutes past the hour you had lost all respect and begun to consider him as one you take lightly.

Now that you know how others feel and think about you when you are late for an appointment, think of the effect this has on your image as a responsible individual. No amount of *"I'm sorry I'm late,"* will ever recover the damage. Show up on time and be considerate of other people's time.

Say it straight

When you say something, mean it and say it straight. Don't underestimate and double-talk a customer; most often it backfires on you. Be a straight shooter.

Don't wait for them to call you. Get a head start.

Once a company has been awarded a contract, it's expected to take full charge. The managerial team has to keep an eye on the job's progress. He must not wait for the customer to call him. The idle time, from the award until the job goes into full swing is the best time for a contractor to set up and get a head start, especially in alteration work. A contractor should mobilize the job and physically do whatever work he can at his own pace. Remember the customer is not the contractor; the contractor is. The customer will usually call the contractor when he thinks the job is ready for him. At that point, usually he will wish he had been there sooner. Staying attentive to the job's needs prevents costly mistakes. It also builds a good working relationship with the customer.

FOLLOW UP ON PAPERWORK

Timely paperwork processing is as important to contract administration as passing inspections is to construction schedules. Procrastination in this area is common among failing contractors. A contractor's efficiency directly affects job progress and collections.

Compliance with contracts, depending on the owner's requirements, can generate a great deal of paperwork. However, regardless of how much paperwork there is, it is as much a part of the contractor's contractual obligation as is the installation of conduit and wire. The only difference is that a contractor may easily get away from installing a certain work, but he will not get away from processing any paperwork, especially if the customer needs it to satisfy the owner or a bank.

In any business there is no room for procrastination in either aspect of the work. Installation and contract administration are essentials to successful contracting. If the contractor does them efficiently he will have a well balanced, performing company.

MARKETING RESULTS

If we wanted to guess we could safely state that nine out of ten contractors who read this chapter, for one reason or another, would take exception to most of its marketing approaches, especially about clean-up and punctuality. Their minds run off with such thoughts as, *"I always get away with clean-up and stuff like that . . . why bother?"* These individuals undoubtedly will have a similar answer for every exception they take in life.

However, the fact is that large numbers of companies fail and go out of business. And if we speculate one more time with statistics, we can say these companies are the same nine-out-of-ten who think they can get away with that *"stuff,"* and simply refuse to subscribe to good business practices. The remaining one out of ten, those that subscribe to good business practices and sound marketing fundamentals, are bound to succeed.

In conclusion, if a company truly wants success, it must take responsibility and deliver complete contracts, and that includes all the related paperwork. Any other practice is counter-productive. If the contractor feels he can't handle contracts with extensive paperwork, he should decide before he signs the contract, or, for that matter, before he bids on them. A good indication as to the extent of paperwork is the type of owner. If he wants to be certain, he should check the entire bidding document.

Live up to contractual obligations. What a contractor will gain in reputation by far outweighs the few dollars he may save in cheating on trivial *stuff*. He has to think of this cost as a good marketing investment.

In marketing, the main objective is to create demand. In any industry demand is created by accumulating as many favorable impressions as possible with those who are in a position to influence others and those who will directly decide on the next contract award. This is one of the secrets of successful business.

When a contract is awarded, a contractor should seize the moment. With it, and with every other contract he undertakes, he has a unique opportunity to create greater demands for himself and for his company. A contract performed on time is the ultimate and most inexpensive marketing tool by which a contractor can establish himself as a competent and trustworthy contractor.

Chapter 3

THE STARTING POINT

WHERE IT ALL STARTS

It all starts with a sales lead. Regardless of the marketing methods employed by a contractor in promoting his business, the result will always be a lead to potential work.

Each sales lead is a new starting point whose outcome is totally dependent on the contractor's decision to accept or reject it. In making that decision, he must bear in mind that unless he's ready to carry it out to its conclusion, he should not accept it. Accepting a sales lead is a commitment to invest his resources, not to mention his reputation as a reliable contractor, into something whose cost gets progressively larger with the extent of his involvement.

Taking on a sale lead is the start of a new business transaction, a "loop" if you will, which like many business transactions, is worthless unless it has the potential to close into a good sale. If, at any time during the course of the loop, the lead's potential is poor or declines, the contractor should not hesitate; he should quickly close the loop and walk away. If he hesitates, he will not only increase his cost with every passing moment, but will also impose undue disappointment on those he's dealing with. For example, abandoning a sales lead three quarters of the way into its loop, when he could have done so at the start, is wasteful and distracting to all parties concerned, and that includes his own staff.

Therefore, for a contractor to get his business on the road to success there is no better way than to evaluate each sales lead before he takes it on. Sales leads are the roots of his business. A lead develops into a job, and a job into a customer. The customers' quality determines his company's quality and thus his success rate.

The knowledge he'll gain on the many aspects of prospective customers and job procedures will assist him in evaluating sales leads, so he can invest his resources (time, energy, and money) on productive business, rather than on chasing wasteful dead-end prospects.

Before undertaking the task of following up a sales lead, regardless of whether it's for a new or an old customer, a contractor should routinely go through an inquiry checklist, with the following questions being at the top of that list:

- How will I get paid?
- Who is the customer?
- Can I successfully deal with this customer?
- Do I have the finances and organization to deliver a successful job?
- Who is my competition?
- Can I be competitive and still make a profit?
- If all answers are favorable and he decides to take on the sales lead, a contractor should use his best resources and go at it wholeheartedly, but if any answer is unfavorable, then, no matter how

attractive the lead is or whatever justifiable reasons he comes up with, he should not second-guess himself, he should just walk away. If it hurts him, it will only be for a couple of days or until he has found a better lead to invest his resources on.

VULNERABILITY

To reinforce the importance of evaluating sales leads, here are a few compelling thoughts on the subject of vulnerability.

The ranks of contractors include individuals whose optimism goes beyond the norm. As many of them confess, they believe things will get better with each devastating blow they get. For example, if the building collapses, they'll make more money from the insurance claim; and, if the scope of work is changed, they'll make more money from the extra work and so on. At least, that is the way they think.

Along with this trend of thought, these individuals, no matter how many times they get hit, always rebound thinking that the next customer is their best friend with their best interests at heart, ready to pay in full for every job they do. In essence, these individuals have the ability to put aside bad experiences, trust newcomers, and treat every new job as a new start. The only difference between this kind of contractor and the wiser contractors is that these contractors, like gamblers, will have to start from scratch every time they lose until they learn how to operate from facts rather than feelings.

On any given day, anyone can call on this contractor to quote a job, and most likely he will invest his last dollar on doing the job without ever questioning the customer's ability to pay. He will work on the assumption that he has a standard contract signed, whatever that means, and that he will get paid in full, especially if he receives one or two partial payments in the interim.

If you think this is exaggerated or fiction, think again. Every day it happens countless times in our industry. If you never experienced it, the following short story, perhaps, will enlighten you:

A few days into demolition, a construction manager for a national chain restaurant went through the yellow pages and invited various trade contractors to bid his work. Those interested were asked to attend a pre-construction meeting where they could visit the job and examine the bid documents.

At the meeting, the attendees—plumbers, electrical contractors, mechanical contractors and the like—as masters of their trade, each got promising answers to their technical and other questions pertaining to schedules, scope of work, material, specialty items, etc., and after almost a two-hour session they could feel the excitement in the air. Each tradesman, if asked, was ready to start building right then and there.

What makes this typical story compelling is the fact that not one single contractor asked the most important question: "How do I get paid?" and when a wiser contractor finally asked, neither the construction manager nor the owner's representative could readily answer the question. As to the contractors present, most of them thought it were an impertinent question, as payment schedules are standard procedures, and with that question a complete silence set in the room, as if a cardinal rule had been broken. However, when asked again, the construction manager had to call the owner and ask which brought the group to the harsh realization that neither the owner's representative nor the construction manager had given much thought to payment schedules.

Nevertheless, the restaurant was built, regardless of payment conditions, by those who failed to heed the warning and who most likely are still hoping to collect on their final payment.

This is not to insinuate that owners or construction managers go around having jobs built with no intention to pay, even though our carelessness in this regard at times is the biggest temptation to them of all. This is merely to remind you how easily enthusiasm can take a contractor into bad investments.

Going back to our short story, either by rule of thumb or actual checking up, each contractor in that room could have avoided any problems. Those that declined the invitation suffered no losses and went on to better jobs. The optimists are still waiting for their payments, not to mention their profits.

When a contractor attends pre-construction meetings, aside from asking vital business questions, he should pay special attention to the other tradesmen. Their line of questioning can tell him a great deal about them and the type of cooperation he can expect on the job. The expertise and cooperation of other trades in carrying out their work diligently greatly affects the outcome of his work. For example, a bad masonry or mechanical contractor can upset the progress of the job and drastically decrease his productivity.

Checking the other contractors' reputation is part of a contractor's prospective job assessment. When he's asked to bid work, he should not hesitate to ask who the major trades are. It may sound unorthodox, but he should make a few phone calls if he has to, for it is all part of his investigative procedure to prevent problems and assure success in all the jobs he does.

WHO'S YOUR CUSTOMER?

The customer is that person who purchases goods or services from a contractor. If a contractor does a job at City Hall for a given general contractor, his customer is the general contractor, not City Hall. His customer is that individual or firm that hires him to do the work and with whom he has a contract regardless of whether it's written, verbal, or implied. This is a relationship that a contractor should never lose sight of in all his dealings. For example, in the case cited above, if he wants to maintain a legal, moral, and ethical standing, he cannot take orders from City Hall, nor should he bypass the general contractor and deal directly with City Hall.

General Contractor

A customer, therefore, can be anyone with whom a contractor deals directly, from a homeowner to a property manager to a general contractor. In contracting, the most prominent customer he's bound to deal with is the general contractor, and therefore a contractor should learn all he can about his character.

Workable Relationships

The general contractor-subcontractor relationship has to be straight-forward, for both parties have a common goal—making a profit in the construction of the project they contract. However, to earn these profits they depend on each other's abilities to carry out the work. Each must do what he does best, that is, use the tools of his trade in the most profitable and professional way. For our purposes we shall refer to this kind of relationship as a "working relationship."

Understanding this relationship and the relative positions to each other and to the project is what makes winning teams. The general contractor must understand the subcontractor's position, and the subcontractor must understand the general contractor's position. Neither should feel threatened by the other's actions when dispatching their duties, especially when they fall within the contract's legal framework and the industry's standard practices.

As the title implies, the general contractor is the individual or firm who contracts the building of a complete project, most likely on a turnkey basis, and at a fixed cost. His position is relatively risky and demands the respect and support of his subcontractors.

Due to our industry's inherent competition, a general contractor, in order to secure a contract, quite often makes extraordinary concessions to the owner. In a working relationship, subcontractors, when asked, generally will share the burden of these concessions. For contractors are bold people who do not fear bad weather, earthquakes, or the like, nor do they anticipate unforeseen events that can jeopardize the completion of a project on time or upset the anticipated construction cost. They can always do better. (And a good thing too, or no building would have ever been built).

The subcontractor, such as the electrical contractor, is

that individual or firm who carries out a portion of the general contractor's work, and in using managerial skills, attempts to make the most profit he can.

To reach his goal, however, he must recognize that a good working relationship with the general contractor is vital. For example, if he wants to be adequately compensated for extras or obtain an approval on a substitution for an item of work, he cannot and should not expect the general contractor to prepare his submissions or do the legwork that is often associated with those requests.

In seeking approvals for substitutions, perhaps the contractor and his supplier are the experts and the only parties interested in its outcome. And, if the outcome is important to him, then no one but himself should handle the details and presentations required by most submittals.

With regard to additions or deletions of work, a contractor should submit change orders on time. Change orders should be complete, including explanatory notes detailing the reason for change and estimate breakdowns justifying the cost.

This clear method will empower and encourage his

teammate, the general contractor, to go to battle with the owner not only for the contractor, but for himself; for he has given him tools with which he too can profit.

Anything short of these methods will only jeopardize whatever profits a contractor is entitled to make on these change orders.

To approach these procedures differently—for example, to merely ask the field superintendent to process them—would probably result in a forgotten promise. This can create a real disappointment later on when the contractor finally realizes that he's not getting paid for the extra work and he has lost all bases for a timely and legitimate claim.

As a subcontractor, a contractor must assume the responsibility to document his work properly and submit what has to be submitted to the general contractor in a timely fashion. There is no room for procrastination in these transactions, especially with the ones that have to do with protecting his own interest— his business.

Basically, this is the respect and relationship that should and must exist between general contractor and subcontractor. Often, regardless of needs and conditions, some relationships are best not started. There are no plausible excuses for knowingly entering a lopsided relationship. If for no other reason, a contractor should be selective of the general contractor he chooses to work with because he will have a great influence over the profit a contractor makes on his investment.

The subordination to the general contractor presumably is motivated by the contractor's optimistic view of the greater number of opportunities he has to generate a higher percentage of profit than the general contractor. But, whatever the view or motive is, a contractor must not lose sight of the general contractor's direct control over moneys due to him. In most cases, the general contractor has the upper hand and can and will cut into the contractor's profit by back-charging whatever expenses he thinks the contractor owes him—the core of much litigation, many disappointments, and many failures.

Perhaps here, in this unbalanced formula of equity and anticipated profits, lies the mystery of what makes most of these relationships work. Leadership and subordination perhaps could be additional reasons.

Regardless of the answer, a contractor must recognize a bad relationship before it starts and prevent it by following his intuition and looking for work elsewhere.

Non-Workable Relationships

Non-workable relationships, for our purpose, are those relationships that, quite often, make us question our judgment and make our discontent grow to unbearable levels. Unworkable relationships also have the tendency to make bank accounts plunge toward dangerous balances.

In theory, however, if a contractor's estimates are the true reflection of anticipated costs and he is able to carry out the work contracted, then the job can be classified as a good job. And if he and the general contractor pay steadfast attention to what is agreed on, then the relationship can also be classified good and, therefore, workable.

Simply put, that is the theoretical aspect of a good job and a workable relationship. Workable, that is, until the unscrupulous human element takes over the relationship.

The introduction of this human element into the

equation requires the contractor to be alert. In today's business, the following two elements concern the contractor most:

The Unscrupulous General Contractor

The unscrupulous general contractor is the first to come to mind. Sooner or later he will cross the contractor's path. And when he does, his actions will leave him with a long-lasting negative impression.

His unscrupulous behavior toward the contractor is frequently encouraged by the contractor's seemingly vulnerable financial position.

To assist the contractor in identifying, and possibly preventing, some of the most unscrupulous contracting methods, the following list has been compiled. While we are aware that, occasionally, some of these practices come about inadvertently, nevertheless we must recognize them here:

- Requesting a quote on an incomplete set of drawings.
- Withholding bidding documents from the bidding package.

- The usage of lopsided contracts, instead of standard industry-accepted contracts.

- The showing of others' bids to lure the contractor into lowering his price.

- Withholding full 10% retainer on payment when theirs was reduced to 5% at the midpoint of the project.

- Unduly cutting down the contractor's monthly requisition.

- Evading and delaying the issuance of bona fide directives and change orders.

- Improper documents signing.

- Withholding items of work, so as to hold up final inspections that will entitle the sub-contractor to collect his moneys.

- Refusal of certified mail.

- Some other items of concern to us affect job site productivity. These items arise from poor field coordination and a general contractor's procedural negligence:

- Unnecessary cluttering of floor space with premature delivery of building materials or fixed fixtures that hinder free movement of rolling scaffolds and similar equipment. This is done merely to save the general contractor on some rental storage trailer.

- Improper field supervision and coordination of trades.

Unscrupulous Plans and Specifications Writers

Conflicts between plans, specifications, and contract documents are usually accidental but still costly when they go undetected during the estimating stages of a project. However, accidental conflicts that are generated by designers, specification writers, and project managers due to their lack of knowledge or responsibility should also be classified as unscrupulous contracting. (For more on this subject and how to prevent it, see Chapter 8, "Protecting the Contract.")

Chapter 4

WHERE TO LOOK FOR WORK

FORESIGHT

This chapter is about how to find work for both the beginning and the seasoned contractor. If a contractor has read and subscribed to the methods introduced in the previous chapters, he should be ready and anxious to apply his newly acquired marketing skills, eager to pick and choose customers and jobs, and, when conditions don't fit his needs, he should have the conviction to walk away; for that's the way he should feel—eager and confident.

However, for a contractor to live by his convictions he

must look at his market opportunities overview—the full picture—and feel comfortable with its prospective outcome. When he can see that, not only will he be able to live by his convictions, but he'll become a focused contractor with only one purpose—success.

It is this foresight that will help a contractor look for and find the work that best fits his marketing plans. If his sight is restricted, as it is many times by limited knowledge of what's around him or by self-imposed limitations, then he's doomed to fail, or at best struggle along just making ends meet.

If a contractor needs a clear demonstration of what we are talking about in this chapter, he can get it by making a very small investment. On a clear night he should take a short helicopter ride over his city, and suddenly he'll see and feel with a sense of brilliancy all the prospective work awaiting him. He'll see street lighting, sports fields, cinemas, malls, shopping centers, sewer treatment plants, substations and switching stations, hospitals, churches, government centers, and the empty lots people will build on. He'll see the extent of his prospective work and, as advocated in this manual, the reason to be choosy, for he has the talent to sell and the know-how to repair, maintain, alter and install all that he sees.

It is with this panoramic sight in mind that we present the following methods and approaches to help the contractor pick and choose his prospective customers and jobs. A contractor can always come back to this list of opportunities to keep his marketing goals sharp and vivid in his mind.

In the following sections we shall cover the many market approaches to Service and Contracting Work.

SERVICE WORK

Service work, as defined here, is the most common type of work for commercial and residential accounts, and it is the most sought out work by start-up contractors. Service work consists of repair, addition, alteration and maintenance of existing installations. This type of work can be generated either by the private sector (for example, Realtors, property managers, home and business owners) or by governmental agencies, such as federal, state, county and municipal. Regardless of what category a contractor chooses, he must always remember that repeat business comes from loyal customers (accounts), and they can only be built by word-of-mouth recommendations. Each satisfied customer will earn the contractor that recommendation, which is the foundation of his service work.

THE ESTABLISHMENT

In recent years both private and public sector service work producers for contractors have been switching from total patronage of service companies to a three-bids system for all work other than emergency work. While this method creates more opportunities in which the contractor may compete, it also imposes on the servicemen's daily schedule. For example, unless a contractor screens and evaluates his sales leads, as discussed in the previous chapter, he'll be giving bids all day long with little success.

In drumming up work, another thing to take into consideration is that no matter how much a customer likes the contractor, or how much work the contractor has done for his company, the award of the next job is always predicated on price first. In other words, a contractor must possess all the qualities a customer will look for in a reliable contractor, with price being always at the top of the list.

PRIVATE SECTOR

While the different methods of generating work from the private sector are generally simple, they can seem unorthodox to some. Nevertheless, the methods introduced here are successful for those that apply them.

To generate service work in the private sector, the contractor's approach is different than in contracting. For example, a contractor may knock on doors at an industrial park, or select any or all the following methods:

Directories

Directories such as Yellow Pages, Community Industrial Listings, and the like, when properly explored, are comparable to the helicopter ride mentioned earlier: through their pages a contractor may shop for his business markets, if you will. For example, if he's a one-man show, just starting out, and wants to create an immediate clientele with good cash flow, choose retailers of lighting fixtures, paddle fans, heat pumps, exhaust fans, spas, major appliances, and he should personally call on them for their electrical needs on a regular basis. If he's beyond starting out, and wishes to expand his service business, then choose home improvement contractors, interior decorators, heating and air conditioning contractors, etc. If he's a well-established contractor with a service work quota to fill, then he should get his sales forces to shop through the industrial pages for suppliers of specialty equipment for offices and businesses such as automotive spray booths, electric car lifters, electronic systems, moveable partitions installers, network computer specialists—and don't forget the insurance adjuster for flood and fire damages—and offer them his expertise services.

In essence, if a contractor is in business, he has to use his imagination and exploit these directories to his advantage as they contain a wealth of markets for the electrical contractor. They are the most informative and inexpensive way to either start up or boost your business, especially when his marketing skills are applied with enthusiasm and determination, for they will pyramid into endless opportunities.

Yellow Pages and Local Directories

In some areas such as the American suburbs, ads placed in Yellow Pages and local directories do not generate as much service work as they used to before the do-it-yourself concept was popularized by Home Depot and building-supply stores. The cost of non-productive ads, especially in long-term commitments, can well overrun small companies' budgets.

After a contractor has taken into consideration the pros and cons and he feels he must advertise in these directories, he should do so on a trial basis. To do this, use a dedicated telephone number for each locality in which you wish to advertise. This method, which is encouraged by many publishers of telephone directories, will allow the contractor to cancel his monthly charges as soon as he shuts off the telephone number used in the ads.

A contractor should not use his advertising telephone number for any other purpose than advertising. His business cards and stationery should have his company's operating telephone numbers, thus directing his new customers to communicate with his office over those lines. Later on, if he decides to shut down the ad he'll be able to retain whatever customers he paid for.

Other hints to consider when placing these ads:

- **Size of Ad-** Larger or largest is not necessarily better. A contractor should look into four or five back issues (the library has them) of the directory he wants to advertise in and check how many ads of the size he's contemplating have survived more than two or three issues. Most likely, if the ad is three quarters of a page or larger, economics will restrict it to no more than two years.

- **Stay With the Crowd-** In any one directory there always is the largest, the smallest, and the in-between ad. The last is where the crowd is most likely to shop. Consumer habits will force the shopper to flip to the next pages for more choices. Page one with only one ad has the consumer cornered and scared of price gouging to pay for the large ad. After flipping over the page, the consumer will tend to stop in the middle, where there are the most choices. If the middle has one-quarter-page ads, he or she will have eight choices and will totally forget page one and all others in between, no matter what their messages are.

- **The Ad Layout-** It must be kept simple and free of clutter. For cost-effective ads, the contractor should review the specifications in Chapter 2, and use them as guidelines here. And use words that sell.

- **The Calls-** A contractor must remember these ads will only generate telephone calls; it is up to him or his staff to be there to receive them and turn them into jobs.

Knocking On Doors

This method can begin at the contractor's next-door neighbor's house and end at the door steps of the largest corporations. It all depends on how ambitious he is and how far he's willing to travel. Regardless of his goal, this method has passed the test of time. In a sense, a contractor may call it business politics at its best. He simply mingles with and lobbies, if you will, those who are most apt to give him work. For a list of who's who, their contact names, mailing addresses, telephone numbers and all pertinent information, he may subscribe to several specialized publications. The companies a contractor will most concentrate on in this endeavor are national chain stores, restaurants, fast-food stations, banks, department stores, and the like that are still entertaining the concept of service contracts for their outlets.

PUBLIC SECTOR

No contractor should be in business without seeking a share of public work. His participation in public works, especially service work, is as essential as joining the local chamber of commerce, or any electrical association. Doing work for the local municipal agencies, besides enhancing the contractor's image as a reliable contractor, generates steady work for his company—sort of a security blanket for when the private construction market slows down. These are markets a contractor must always cultivate, for they are the bedrock of his business.

It is a common temptation for most contractors, however, as soon as they get busy with private work, to abandon all sales efforts for public work. This demonstrates that these contractors have not evaluated their marketing plans, or the consequences of quitting.

Many public agencies keep a list of bidders to whom invitations-to-bid documents are sent. For a contractor to maintain his position on these lists, as most of them are extensive, he must be responsive when he's invited. If not, after a period of time, usually a year, or a certain number of no-responses, he'll be dropped from the list—an event that will not favor him the next time he's looking for work with that agency.

The process of becoming an accepted contractor, from the filing of applications until he is regularly invited to bid work by the various government agencies (aside from the so-called lottery or rotation system you'll hear about) will take some doing on his part, requiring perseverance and performance. As in the private sector, when doing service work for public agencies, a contractor must build a solid reputation for dependability. If he pays close attention to their needs and completes the work on time and as specified, contract administrators will naturally begin to favor him in their next round of invitations. In other words, he'll be pulled out of the list of prospective bidders and added to the list of responsive and dependable contractors. When that occurs, he will have closed a business loop successfully, for work will be looking for him, instead of him looking for work.

A contractor should remember that this is service work he is looking for in the public sector, where most agencies are authorized to award work without competitive bidding, up to a certain amount. A contractor should find out what those limits are with each agency for which he intends to work. To apply, a contractor need not visit any of these agencies. He can begin by calling the purchasing agent or the contracting administrator of the specific agency he's interested in, and have them send him the necessary documents to place him on their bidder's list. A contractor should study the material he receives from each agency. Each operates under a different set of rules and regulations.

Public Agencies

For a complete list of public agencies within his locality, a contractor may start with the white pages of the telephone directories and end at the Small Business Administration office. The following lists are meant to steer him in the right direction. A contractor should investigate any other areas or agencies that might interest him.

Government Agencies

Government agencies that are most apt to provide service work are:

- General Service Administration (GSA). Manages all properties owned and leased by the US Government such as post offices, office buildings, etc.

- Federal Aviation Administration (FAA). Responsible for all navigation and landing systems for private airports, including structures that house said systems.

- US Army Corps of Engineers

- US Navy

- Housing and Urban Development (HUD)

State Agencies

- Department of Transportation

- General Service Administration

- Department of State

County Agencies

- Board of Education

- Public Library

- Treatment Plants

- Hospitals

Municipal Agencies

- Public Works
- Recreational Facilities
- Housing Authorities
- Utilities

CONTRACTING WORK

Construction Reports

On a given day all sorts of prospective work can be funneled through construction reports right to the contractor's doorstep, or, thanks to electronic media, to his desktop computer without his traveling a single mile. Through these reports a contractor is able to feel the pulse of his industry in any locality he wishes. The frequency and age of the information he chooses to receive comes with a price tag that varies with style, territory, and immediacy. However, none of these services, when properly fitted to his business budget, will ever exceed the cost of sending his sales forces into the field.

A contractor can be informed on a daily or weekly basis of who's planning and designing what, and who's building where and when, or who won and lost yesterday's bids, with a complete list of bidders, their telephone and facsimile (fax) numbers, addresses and other pertinent information he'll need to bid the job he chooses.

While these reports are available to the contractor through private companies as well as through various governmental agencies, their final product is the same. They produce sales leads which a contractor must investigate before he puts his wheels in motion, as he would any other sales lead.

SALES APPROACH

In contracting, cold calls are seldom productive, and cold calls made at the wrong time of the day are never productive. The most effective time to contact a prospective customer, especially a general contractor who's on the go, traditionally is between 7:00 and 10:00 a.m. That is the time when we all think most clearly and are most receptive to doing business. In our industry that is the time of the day when most deals are made; for the rest of the day is spent on job management and negotiations with those we called early in the morning. For example, knocking at a general contractor's door at two in the afternoon on a fishing expedition for work, without even a job name to allow the contractor's foot-in-the-door, will greatly decrease his odds, for this is a cold and wasteful sales call.

When looking for work, a contractor should take two things into consideration: (1) The time of day he's making the sales call, and (2) the knowledge of the job he's calling about. The second of these is a vital element of his sales call. The more knowledgeable he is about the job he seeks, the more confident his prospective customer will feel about him, and the better his chances of winning the job. At first, a contractor may acquire part of that knowledge through construction reports, and later complement it through his estimating process.

In summary, a contractor should look for contracting work through whatever means he chooses, and then follow its progress from designing to bidding stages, attaining the list of bidders and finding the right time to contact those he wishes to work with. Once he has gotten his commitments, he can then enter the race by estimating and bidding on the job. This simple process depends on the contractor's sales lead analysis and is the reason why he should never call on a general contractor without a specific project in mind in which both of them have a common interest.

Contracting With Public Agencies

In some areas, mechanical trades for public jobs are bid through general contractors; in others, directly to the owner. However, no matter what system is adopted in an area, the basic bidding principle remains the same. Therefore, when a contractor is looking for work and he does not wish to subscribe to paid reports and bid for work that is directly bid to the owner, then he may want to apply to the various governmental agencies of his choice and ask to be placed on their bidders mailing lists. In this case he should follow the same guidelines laid out earlier under the Service Work section.

When to Look For Work

A contractor should look for work when he is busy. He should not fall for the "I am too busy to look for work," syndrome, nor should he get distracted from sales by the first job he gets. Eventually he will complete it, and he'll be looking for work again, this time under pressure, and he will have lost his marketing momentum.

Chapter 5

THE BID PRICE

PRESENTATION

Once a bid is compiled, it would be counterproductive to lose a job due to a weak presentation. Weak presentations are the hallmark of those who lack confidence in their estimates and consequently in their bid prices, thus reflecting this weakness all the way into their proposal and presentation. The fact that a contractor burned the midnight candle or knows the customer well does not exonerate him from presenting a businesslike proposal.

A clear-cut proposal is the hallmark of a successful businessperson who radiates confidence. Confidence is, of course, the foundation of a sound business relationship. Remember, most of us would like to know, in the least number of words, exactly what we're getting for our money. When certainty is lacking, so is confidence. For example, *"The work will cost you between $2,000 and $3,000"* is a sure loser to *"The work will cost you $2,700 with the following exceptions"* complemented by a clear list of exceptions. Even if the first statement is well meant and the job's ultimate cost may be less than $2,700, the second statement wins because it delivers confidence. The statement satisfies the customer's objective—firmly knowing where he or she stands beforehand.

When a contractor is invited to quote a job, people want firm prices. If he's not sure about the job and needs to add some contingencies into his price, he should do it with confidence, regardless of consequences. When a contractor shows uncertainty he's telling the customer that he doesn't know what he's doing. While this is an innate syndrome with doubtful individuals, it is amazingly common, and at times habitual, among well intentioned contractors. Every now and then it just creeps up on them to kill a few good jobs. A contractor should review his quotation pattern, and if he's guilty he should take corrective actions.

PRICING STRUCTURE

The oldest and hardest barrier to overcome is the psychological effect the less-than-a-dollar pricing structure has over the consumer. For instance, $1.99 is not $2.00, just as $99,999.99 is not $100,000.00. If a contractor analyzes this principle and adapts it to his quotations and change orders pricing, it can make a great deal of difference in his business bottom line, especially if he's an average contractor doing lots of small jobs.

When pricing jobs, a contractor wants his number to deliver the most favorable impact while getting as many dollars as he can without jeopardizing the chances of getting the job. Because there has to be a number at which a contractor must freeze his bid price, cutting it may well give him the clearest and highest price he can get.

If the bid, for example, adds up to $10,050.25, the

contractor should make it clearer by rounding it off to $10,050. In lump-sum bids, he should always round off his price to the next full dollar. Now, though he has made it easier to read, it's still too high and will not favor him. According to our marketing principle, the number is exactly $51 too high—an amount most contractors will gladly shave off their bid price just to get the job. The bid should be $9,999 or, if he feels funny about all the nines, $9,990. No matter how he looks at it, psychologically his new bid price appears to be far cheaper than it really is and less cumbersome than the original $10,050.25.

By doing this, he should break the barrier between $10,000 and $9,000, where the in-between numbers from 9,001 to 9,999 or from 10,001 to 10,999 have little or no effect on the initial price-impact. For example, unless he's engaged in fierce competition, bidding the job at $9,250 or $9,450 or $9,750 or $9,999 or any other number in the $9,000 range will not take him out of the customer's $9,000 cost-perception. The $9,000 becomes the leading number in his bid and any other bid above his, even by a dollar, will fall into the next plateau, the $10,000 cost-perception. And if, as advocated here, the proposal is written with certainty and clarity, a contractor will be placing most of the odds in his favor.

One further point to note is that once a contractor has decided on which plateau to bid the job, further cutting the bid price or staying at the bottom end of that plateau does not greatly enhance his chances of getting the job. In fact, he can speculate his bid price all the way down to close to nothing and still have no chance. The contractor's judgment of the competition and his knowledge of the customer are the best tools that can guide him in this endeavor. However, it's worth noting that if a contractor contracts, say, eight jobs per month and drops an average of $500 per job, he need not be an accountant to know the effect it will have on his bottom line. Being a low bidder is what our business is about, but being too low a bidder most of the time is an unnecessary burden.

A contractor should be attentive to this subtle principle, for after all it is not so subtle. Major corporations use it in their national marketing campaigns to lead the public to believe that they are offering lower prices when in reality they are using the higher end of their pricing structure.

WHAT ARE YOUR ODDS?

The odds are what a contractor makes them. Why should his bid be favored over another? A long list of answers may apply, but the most logical are lower price, reputation, and perseverance, with perseverance leading the pack.

Diligently following the development of a bid and providing the customer with the necessary estimating support from the moment a contractor accepts the invitation to its completion is a sure way to place the odds in his favor. The support referred here mainly consists of the timely submission of a written quote, attending pre-construction conferences, and a genuine concern for the job.

A written proposal can be submitted well before the bid date. A contractor can, and should, submit its outline, short of the price, soon after he begins estimating the job. Aside from his standard terms and conditions, it should list the scope of work and exceptions, a task done with a standard form giving his prospective customer ample time to digest the bulk of the bid. At bid date, the only thing left for the contractor to do should be to call in the price. Employing this method most likely will maintain a favored place for the contractor in his customer's preferred bidders list.

CHANGING THE BASIC PRICE STRUCTURE

In this chapter, the subject of fine-tuning the bidding price—for example, from one plateau to another—should not be confused with a fundamental change of the estimating pricing structure. Developing a specific pricing structure that keeps a contractor competitive and profitable is the result of a painstaking process. Once developed, the pricing structure is the contractor's foremost resource, and therefore it should be exempt from any tampering or speculation.

The bidding price should always be compiled from the estimated cost and the company library of markups and not from hearsay, guessing, or gut feeling numbers. Pursuing over-inflated bids, even when a contractor gets few jobs, ultimately will destroy his ability to compete in a realistic world. And when push comes to shove, a contractor will be out of the mainstream.

Chapter 6

THE CONTRACT

STANDARD CONTRACT FORMS

The multitude of standard contract forms used in the construction industry today makes it impractical, if not impossible, to list them all in one chapter. While the most common were originally accepted as fair and impartial, thanks to the imagination of the overprotective or unscrupulous customer, they have evolved into detrimental legal instruments from which we must protect ourselves.

What follows, therefore, is a collection of the most

elaborate contract clauses a contractor is likely to encounter. These contract clauses are quoted unaltered as they appear in various executed contracts. Each abstract is identified by a letter, and key words or phrases that adversely affect the spirit of the clause are printed in bold. Any comment that follows a clause is intended to give the contractor a sense of how to avoid these and other similar legal traps. In the process he'll learn how to promptly recognize and spot these "sore spots" in his contract readings.

ABSTRACT "A"

Payments

- If the Owner does not pay the Contractor **for any reason**, including the Owner's insolvency, the Contractor has no obligation to pay the Subcontractor.

Comment: What if the contractor is negligent in carrying out the work? Should he be exonerated from all obligations?

Change Orders

- Only changes authorized in writing and agreed to in amount prior to performance by the Contractor will be paid. It is agreed that if such change involves an order, directive, act or omission of the Owner, or any other third party, then the Subcontractor shall be limited in recovery to the amount received by the Contractor from said third party, **less its costs, markup, expenses, and attorney fees**.

Comment: What we can gather here is that the general contractor wants to make his profit and more, but would not allow the sub to make a profit. In fact he's going to charge the sub all his expenses plus legal fees even if he only chooses to consult his lawyer for whatever reason.

Completion

- Work will be completed on or before 00/00/00. **Time is of the essence.**

Comment: When a contractor encounters *"Time is of the essence,"* bells should ring, for this phrase has a specific legal significance. The customer is alerting the contractor that the satisfactory completion and acceptance of the contract is contingent on the completion of the work on time. If the contract is not completed in time, then the contract has no existence or value.

Termination

- (a) Should there be any work stoppage or slowdown caused by a strike, picketing, boycott, or any other voluntary or involuntary cessation, delay or interference of work by the Subcontractor, or the Subcontractor's suppliers, or any of them for any reason, and which, **in the judgment of the Contractor** is causing or **is likely to cause** delay in the progress of the work to be done by the Subcontractor, the Contractor shall have the right to declare this Agreement in default in accordance with the procedures outlined in Sub-Paragraph (c) of this Paragraph 4."

- (b) All work under this subcontract shall conform to all applicable laws, rules, regulations and codes. Wherever the specifications or drawings conflict with such documents, **work shall be performed in compliance therewith at no extra cost.** Subcontractor further agrees that [it] shall comply with the Occupational Safety and Health Act of 1970 as amended and all rules, regulations, standards and orders issued there under. If any act or failure by the Subcontractor results in the assessment of a civil penalty against the Contractor, Subcontractor shall reimburse Contractor the amount paid by Contractor on demand by Contractor. **If, in the opinion of Contractor,** Subcontractor is in violation of any standard, rules, regulations, or code requirements of said OSHA Act, Contractor shall have the right to declare this Agreement in default in accordance with the procedures outlined in Sub-paragraph (c) of this Paragraph 4."

- (c) In the event that Contractor **desires** to declare this Agreement in default for any reasons stated in Sub-Paragraph (a) or (b) above, or in the event that Subcontractor threatens to or fails in any manner to properly or timely perform any obligation on its part to be performed under this Agreement, Contractor shall have the right to declare this Agreement in default after giving the subcontractor twenty-four hours notice of the intention of the Contractor to claim such default. . . .

Comment: These clauses, which unfortunately are becoming very common, should warn a contractor to read carefully, especially the bold typeface writing, and then decide how far he is willing to commit himself.

Subcontractor Representation

- The Subcontractor shall have a representative competent in the field of work covered under this Agreement on the job site at all times work under this Agreement is being performed. Said representative shall have full authority to act on Subcontractor's behalf and **shall not be changed without written consent of the Contractor**.

- Subcontractor agrees to indemnify and hold Contractor harmless from any and all liability, claims and damages, including attorney fees, which any party might seek or claim against the Contractor, or which it may incur, and which directly or indirectly, actively or passively, was caused by Subcontractor or one in its employ, contract, or for whom the Subcontractor might be responsible. Subcontractor's liability and indemnification shall be valid whether or not the Contractor was directly or indirectly responsible for the damage or was otherwise liable to the third party.

ABSTRACT "B"

Contractor-Subcontractor Relationship

- Contractor shall have the same rights and privileges as against the Subcontractor herein as the Owner in the General Contract has against the Contractor.

- **Subcontractor acknowledges that he has read the General Contract** and all drawings and specifications, and is familiar therewith and agrees to comply with and perform all provisions thereof applicable to the Subcontractor.

- The Subcontractor agrees to indemnify and hold harmless the Contractor and the Owner from and against any and all suits, claims, actions, losses, costs, penalties, and damages of whatever damage kind or nature, **including attorney's fees arising** out of, in connection with, or incident to the Subcontractor's performance of the subcontract work.

Comment: While this Hold Harmless clause appears to be milder than the one in Abstract "A" it is very bold when considering it was part of a $1500 contract—a steep liability to assume when the cost of attorney's fees for any claim can well be ten times the contractor's anticipated profit.

As subcontractor, a contractor must keep these clauses in proportion to the contract amount and his anticipated profit. A contractor should think! How can he prevent anyone from suing the owner for a defective device the contractor did not manufacture? How can he then indemnify the owner and the general contractor for something that is specified by the owner and manufactured by someone over whom he has no control? You make the final call.

- In the event that any work fails to conform to the requirements of the contract, the same shall be corrected by the Subcontractor immediately upon its discovery; further, in the event that defects due to faulty materials or workmanship appear within one year from **useful occupancy,** the Subcontractor shall at his own expense correct the same and this applies to work done by his Subcontractor(s), his employees and those working by, through, or under him.

- The work covered by this contract shall be commenced within three (3) days after written notice to the Subcontractor by the Contractor, and completed within 60 days from date of commencement: **time being of the essence** of this contract. Loss of time on account of materials or work being condemned will not be considered as a cause for an extension of the contract time. In the event the Subcontractor fails to complete on time, he shall pay the Contractor by way of liquidating damages the sum of $300 per day for each and every day the work remains incomplete unless the cause for delay is caused by strikes not caused by Subcontractor, fire, governmental regulations, or acts of God, in which case the time for completion shall be extended for the actual time of such delay. Said liquidated damages shall be deducted as such from balance due the Subcontractor. Should damages exceed the sum due, or to become due, the Subcontractor, then in that event, shall be liable unto the Contractor for such difference.

Comment: Again, $300 per day on a $1,500 contract?

- Should the Subcontractor fail to do or perform the work required hereunder, thereby in the **opinion** of the Contractor causing or threatening to cause delay in the general progress of the work, Contractor shall have the right to declare this Contract to be breached by the Subcontractor and cancel this Contract by notice to him in writing and to re-negotiate and re-execute contract(s) for the completion of the work required to be done under their Contract with such persons, firms, or corporations as shall in the **opinion** of the Contractor be necessary. In the event Contractor cancels the Contract, as hereinabove provided, it shall pay to the Subcontractor only for work completed to the date of the cancellation and the Subcontractor shall not be entitled to profits of any kind or character, anticipated or otherwise, or compensation for materials and labor unfurnished. Further, all losses, damages, and expenses, including attorney's fees in the prosecution or defense of any action or suit incurred by or resulting to Contractor on the above account shall be borne by and charged against Subcontractor, the Contractor may recover on said bond, and both Subcontractor and/or his surety agree to pay

Contractor immediately such losses, damages, expenses, and attorney's fees.

Comment: In this clause a contractor is at the mercy of the customer's opinion, and not of accepted business practice.

- The Contractor shall not be responsible or accountable for any losses or damages that shall or may happen to the Subcontractor's work, materials tools, or equipment employed during construction until **all work is completed and accepted by Owner.**

Comment: What does it mean "until completed"? Would he pay then for damages?

- The Subcontractor shall put himself in communication with other subcontractors whose work may affect his, so as to promote harmony of work. In the event Subcontractor, its agents, employees, or subcontractors commits or allows to be committed any act or acts, or does or allows to be done anything(s) which tends to create or creates disharmony, a work slowdown, work stoppage, or strike, then and in that event **the Contractor shall have the absolute right to**

immediately cancel this Contract and complete same in accordance with breach of contract procedure as set forth in Section 10.

• All labor employed by the Subcontractor upon the job-site will be subject to the Contractor's approval and in the event the Contractor finds fault with any employee **for any reason whatsoever**, said employee shall immediately be removed from the job-site and replaced.

Comments: For any reason "whatsoever." Can a contractor afford the customer chasing his workers away?

• The work shall be done subject to the final approval of Contractor and Architect, if any, and their decision as to the performance of the work in accordance with the drawings and specifications and the true construction and meaning of same shall be final.

INDEPENDENT CLAUSES COLLECTED FROM VARIOUS CONTRACTS:

Payment Sample 1

- The Contractor shall submit to the Owner's Representative, before the Owner's Representative shall be required to make any payments, an application for each payment and receipts or vouchers showing his payments for materials and labor and a schedule of the various parts, including quantities, and supported by such evidence as to its correctness as the Owner's Representative may require; and the Owner shall at all times be entitled to retain 10% of all moneys due and owing to the Contractor as part security for the faithful performance of this agreement, said 10% so withheld shall not be paid to the Contractor until 30 days after final acceptance of the work or materials **shall have been made by the owner.**

Comment: What if the owner never accepts?

Payment Sample 2

- Project is to be invoiced at completion of project. A notarized Waiver of Lien must be submitted with Subcontractor's invoice. Approved Change Orders are to be invoiced separate from the contract amount and a separate lien waiver must be submitted. **No invoice will be processed for payment until a lien waiver** and certificate of insurance is received. Two payments will be issued: first for 90% of the contract amount and second for retention and approved Change Orders. Payment for properly submitted invoices will be made within five (5) days after Contractor's receipt of payment from Owner.

Comment: If in order to get paid a contractor must release his rights to lien, then why bother with lien laws in the first place?

WORKING CONDITIONS:

- Working hours are 12AM to 12PM or as approved by the superintendent.

Comments: Under this clause a contractor will have a tough time collecting overtime or any other premium time.

POSSESSION PRIOR TO COMPLETION

- Whenever it may be useful or necessary for the Contractor to do so, **the Contractor shall be permitted to occupy and/or use any portion of the work** which has been either partially or fully completed by the Subcontractor before final inspection and acceptance thereof by the Owner, but such use and/or occupation shall not relieve the Subcontractor of his guarantee of said work and materials nor of his obligation to make good at his own expense any defect in materials and/or workmanship which may occur or develop prior to Contractor's release from responsibility to the Owner. Provided, however, the Subcontractor shall not be responsible for the maintenance or such portion of the work as may be used and/or occupied by the Contractor, nor for any damage thereto that is due to or caused by the negligence of the Contractor during such period of use or occupancy.

Comment: The ceiling electrical rough is completed before the ceiling grid is installed and the owner ships all wall cabinet units. He invokes this clause, storing the cabinet units in the middle of the floor. When the grid is finally installed the contractor is asked to install the lighting fixture. The difference now is that the contractor cannot use rolling scaffolds and his crew has to work on 12-foot step ladders. If a contractor puts in a claim for it, the customer will reject it, for he says the contractor is not entitled to extra compensation. What do you think? Can the contractor prevent this from happening to himself? Yes! The contractor should be aware of the existence of this clause and then have it struck out before he accepts the job.

Owner's Furnished Materials

- Subcontractor shall be responsible for unloading, storing, maintaining, and inventorying any Owner supplied material and equipment pertinent to his trade. Written notice shall be given to the Contractor within 24 hours of any shortages or damage of Owner supplied material and equipment. **Failure to notify Contractor of shortage or damage within 24 hours** constitutes acceptance by the Subcontractor and the Subcontractor will assume responsibility for shortage and damage.

Comment: The only problem with this clause is that most owner-supplied materials arrive well in advance of schedule and the super or the owner doesn't want any boxes open until installation time. Have the clause struck out or the deadline extended to installation time.

Extra Work Clauses:

- If the Owner requests changes by altering, adding or deducting from the work to be performed under this contract, the Contractor shall give the Owner's Representative a written proposal outlining work to be performed, including cost of the labor, materials and equipment, which shall be approved by the Owner's Representative, in writing, before the Contractor proceeds to execute the work, and in any event the Contractor shall not be entitled to any claims of extras unless approved by Owner's Representative in writing. **Extra charges shall not be claimed by the Contractor due to weather conditions or job scheduling.**

Comments: The last sentence takes away the spirit of the clause, which is fair compensation for extra charges. What if the general contractor chooses to schedule work in such a way that it will impair the contractor's productivity far below his estimate? Should he be compensated?

POINTERS AND OBJECTIVES

Remember these are suggestions based on the legal doctrine that most courts of law accept. For specific and legal advice on these points of law a contractor should always consult his lawyer.

Construction Drawings- When a contractor receives a set of drawings, there is an implied guarantee by the owner that the drawings are correct and suitable to carry out the work. This is why a contractor cannot hold liable the architect, the engineer, or other professionals, except the owner. The only time a contractor can hold the architect or other professionals liable is when the damage involves injuries to others or to property. All other losses, such as money loss, contractors' loss of productivity, etc., are not binding to their performance.

Architects- Most architects are supervisory architects with limited control. Before a contractor tries to sue an architect, it is wise to know that in most cases recourse to professionals is a limited right and the "economic loss rule" applies. The owner is liable for defective design.

Judges- Clarity of contract is the contractor's best prevention. Most judges are not construction people. And construction disputes can be complex.

Beneficiary to the Contract- A contractor should always find out if there is any beneficiary to the contract he signs. There can be some nasty surprises if the beneficiary is not the person a contractor thought he was dealing with.

Right to stop work- A contractor should always negotiate this clause into his contract: "If not paid within 7 days the subcontractor has the right to stop work." Then if the owner breaks his promise a contractor can stop work.

Requisition- Contract breakdown for requisition by virtue of clarity supports breach of contract. For example, the amount due is better defined. It gives less excuse for the owner not to pay and eliminates ambiguity, which is the cause of disputes.

Arbitration rather than court- When reviewing the contract a contractor should look for this provision. If it is arbitration, is it general arbitration or just for a specific dispute? The difference between court and arbitration is that the court will allow a contractor to call anyone he wants or that has anything to do with the case or dispute, while in arbitration the contract will say how to dispute. If the contract calls for arbitration, the contractor as subcontractor will be subject to arbitration. Arbitration is final; court can be appealed.

Termination and specifics- For example, giving notice. If a contractor wants to preserve his rights, follow the contract procedures to the letter.

Other contracts- The contractor should always check what other contracts or documents are part of or are incorporated in his contract.

Final Payment- The contractor should always negotiate how many punch lists he will be subjected to and whose punch list is final in order to release his payment.

Signatures- Photocopied or faxed signatures are okay until challenged.

CONCLUSION

Before a contractor undertakes a contractual obligation, he must have a clear perspective on these and other elements that entrap the unwary contractor, for the danger of running into crooked dealings will always be there.

A common myth among unwary contractors is their belief in standard contract forms. They are intimidated when exposed to long double-sided pages of small print, leading them to accept any such form as "standard" (whatever standard means) and so long as they are standard, their reasoning goes, it's okay to sign. And so they do. Nowadays, word processors, laser printers, and fancy-bordered color paper can produce the most standard-looking contracts money can buy.

A contractor, to free himself from this form of intimidation, should dissect the contract by first scanning through and highlighting the titles of those clauses that concern him most (If need be, he should review Chapter 3 and the earlier comments here), then he should review their content and underline or annotate his objections to each clause. Upon completion, he should analyze his objections and decide whether he wishes to negotiate the contract or simply walk away (see Chapter 7, "Negotiations").

A contractor should never underestimate the responsibility he assumes and the risk he and his entire staff take when signing a contract. Every one's future or job can be on the line. A clause that may appear trivial or misplaced has no meaning until invoked. A contractor should communicate with his super, estimator, secretary or anyone else involved in the outcome of the contract. A simple thought or suggestion from those he least expects can change things for the better. If there are doubts, a contractor should have such clauses crossed out if possible, and, if not, then he should take legal advice before he signs such an agreement.

All that has been covered so far in this chapter is not meant to paralyze the contractor nor prevent him from signing contracts and taking jobs. On the contrary, it's meant to encourage him to take jobs that he would otherwise walk away from for fear of not understanding the contract. The intention here is to give the contractor the ammunition to be able to negotiate his way into sound and fair contracts and avoid those sure losers.

In our industry the number of good customers far outweighs the number of bad ones. It just happens that the bad ones are easier to reach for they are always on the lookout for new contractors and appear to be greater in number. A contractor's challenge, therefore, is to find those good ones who are tightly held captive by his competition.

Chapter 7

NEGOTIATIONS

MEETING THE CUSTOMER

This is the day a contractor has been longing for, the day of negotiating and signing the job. Negotiating the job, however, goes beyond the legal ramifications of a contract. It involves translating the parties' offer and acceptance into a fair and equitable agreement.

In life, we constantly negotiate for what we want. *"I'll give you this if you give me that."* But wants, most often, come with strings attached. We must exchange things we already have for those things we want. Those that know how to ask and exchange usually get what they're after. In contracting, a contractor must sharpen his natural skills and, beforehand, know what he wants and its relative value (what he is willing to pay or give up for it).

Before we enumerate the most common items a contractor should bargain for when negotiating a contract, let's analyze the reason why he is meeting with the customer. The most obvious reason is that each of them thinks he can deal with the other. In other words, there is a meeting of the minds on two of the three basics of contract: solicitation, offer, and acceptance.

The solicitation, invitation for bid, was accepted by the contractor. The offer, the contractor's bid price, is (almost) acceptable to the customer. And the acceptance of the terms and conditions under which the contract is to be carried out is open for negotiation; that is the basis of the meeting. In order to close the deal, each is willing to give and take a few points.

Going to such a meeting unprepared is counterproductive, to say the least. To no one's surprise, what the customer mostly wants is a lower price and better legal protection. To the surprise of many, the customer, in return, is willing to compromise on the scope of work as well as on the terms and conditions. This opportunity comes once in the life of the contract, and it is before the contractor signs it. Any future modification can only be made through change orders, which usually carry heavier price tags.

An astute contractor should always be ready to negotiate most contracts without a rehearsal. Mastering this skill is quite simple. As a negotiator, a contractor should develop two mental lists: one for the general conditions and one for the scope of work (guidelines for these lists are detailed later on in this chapter). Each list should deal with items that are most likely to be accepted by the customer and that the contractor is willing to trade in for a fair compensation. A contractor should assign to each item a dollar value and use it as a bargaining chip to either get what he wants or to offset any price cutting. Each item's value will determine its negotiating priority.

However, before we proceed with this bargaining concept, we need to clarify one important point. The quoted price must include every item the contractor is putting on the table or he will be giving away moneys that were not allocated in his bid price.

With a little practice a contractor will be in control of all his bargaining chips and always able to get something in return for every dollar he shaves off his bid price.

General conditions:

These items are listed here because they generally favor the writer of the contract document—the customer—whose standard contract form most often is written to protect against an array of circumstances; unless a contractor points out its lopsidedness, it will stay as written. Staying within the spirit of negotiation, the contractor should negotiate toward his corner, or at least to the middle, those items he feels will benefit him most. A contractor will be surprised how many will fall into his corner just for the asking.

- **Method of payment** - Whatever payment schedule a contractor works out is fine as long he doesn't burden his cash flow and as long as the balance due upon physical completion does not exceed 10% of the contract price.

- **Down Payment** - A contractor should use his judgment and should not be too bashful to ask; especially if he thinks the job warrants such a payment.

- **Retainer reduction** - **A** contractor should be aware—most contracts allow the original 10% retainer to be reduced to 5% or less after the job is 50% complete. A contractor should have that stipulated in his contract.

- **Substitutions** - There is no better time to have specified material or equipment substituted than at the negotiating table. Because this can be a high-priced ticket item, a contractor should know his facts and figures beforehand.

- **Special Equipment**
Through this item a well thought-out presentation can pay large dividends.

- **Limit the Change Order Amount**-There are times when large change orders can adversely affect a job. For example, a contractor signed a

$40,000 contract to wire a commercial shell that he now wishes he had not signed. The customer, in accordance with the terms of the contract, issues a change order to wire a tenant space on a time and material basis which is worth $90,000, but, for whatever reason, the contractor doesn't want to do it. The customer can hold him liable for breach of contract, thus jeopardizing the base contract.

To prevent this situation, especially in projects where large change orders are probable, a contractor should evaluate all possibilities and then, if necessary, have a clause added to the contract requiring change order amounts not exceed, say, 30% of the contract amount and giving the contractor the right to refuse if they do.

- **No back charges without notice** - Customers back charging contractors at the end of the job is a common practice that is difficult to fight, especially when the prospect of collecting the final payment is overshadowed by legal fees that can be larger than the amount due. A fair and easy safeguard is to add a clause that reads something like this: *"The customer shall notify the contractor* *of any impending Back Charges at the time they occur. Back Charges shall be treated as Change Orders."*

- **Completion date** - A contractor should bear in mind that the electrician, in most jobs, is the first one in and the last one out. His completion is mostly dependent on others. If a contractor can, he should stay away from fixed dates. They usually breed liquidating damages.

- **Premium time** - This is a very costly item if not clearly defined. A contractor should be careful in his negotiation. In many cases, it can easily get out of control.

- **Surplus Material** - In alteration work, it's always good to know who owns surplus material. A contractor should state it clearly, because it's worthless until a salvage company makes an offer to the customer.

Scope of Work

A contractor should know the cost, when applicable, of

each of the following items before he begins negotiations.

- Survey work: Benchmarks and coordinates
- Concrete cutting and core boring
- Trenching, back-filling, and compacting
- Cutting and patching
- Garbage removal
- Fixture supports
- Lamp installation
- Fireproofing
- Hoisting and warehousing
- Maintenance of temporary light and power

Negotiating fair contracts is an exciting challenge. A good negotiator is always respected and ultimately makes good, lasting friends, especially when he delivers on his promises.

Perspective

When you can assume the viewpoint of the business as a whole, rather than just the viewpoint of an individual worker, you become immensely more valuable and productive. The material in this chapter will help you understand how the business side of most industries works by taking you into the mind of the employer.

Chapter 8

PROTECTING THE CONTRACT

SETTING THE STAGE

Because unscrupulous contracting is as detrimental to our business as cancer is to society, we have to learn how to prevent it, and, if necessary, how to deal with it. It's important to note that while we're most concerned with unscrupulous contracting, disputes can arise in most relationships.

To protect his interests in every job he does, it's better for a contractor to have a standard policy of recording the most prominent events of a business relationship in chronological order from the start than to try to trace events back when the contractual relationship has deteriorated into a dispute and everyone has gone home at the end of the job.

The ultimate answer to a dispute is to dispute it in a court of law. However, the most practical and often the most profitable way is to prevent the dispute before it takes place—that is what this chapter is all about.

It's not the intention of this work, however, to precipitate the contractor into an array of legal maneuvers or into starting a war with his customers. When a contractor adheres to basic policies, he will select and preserve items of contractual importance for his files. And should the need arise, he will have a set of legal documents capable of delivering the one ounce of cure that settles disputes out of court.

DOCUMENTATION

To document the job's most pertinent information, drawings aside, a contractor needs a set of files where information is compiled and maintained for future use. Typically this set consists of:

- Job Folder

- Diary

- Intelligence File

Job folder

An efficient job folder for most contracts is a six-section legal folder. The sections can be labeled as follows:

- Estimate/ Contract / Permits / Correspondence

- Contract Breakdown / Billing

- Pending Change Orders

- Approved Change Orders

- Submittal Pending (Letter of transmittal only. Shop Drawings and the like are filed as drawings.)

- Submittal Approved (Letter of Transmittal Only. Shop Drawings and the like are filed as drawings.)

Diary

The diary, when accurately kept, is the backbone of the contractor's stage-setting procedure. On large jobs with a field office, the diary is kept by the job super or foreman. However, in smaller jobs, where the labor force attendance is periodic, the safest procedure is to keep the diary in the main office and have the lead-men report in at the end of each working day. A contractor should remember that field people have a greater tendency to procrastinate on paperwork and tomorrow, not to mention the day or week after, their recollection of events is not as sharp as it is today. With every passing hour, their recollection can dwindle down to nothing.

The diary should be standardized to include basic topics, giving uniform guidelines to the person making the report and minimizing oversights. A good diary, aside from its obvious advantages for recordkeeping, enables the contractor to follow the job progress and recount each event with accuracy. It can be a very influential record in a court of law.

The most economical and credible diaries are those maintained in inexpensive spiral-bound notebooks. A contractor should maintain one for each job. Each page should bear the same format:

- Date and day of the week
- Weather, including the day's temperature
- Workers' names and hours worked
- Items worked on
- Change orders and directives issued or received, if any

- Material received

- Inspections

- Visitors' names

- Rental equipment received or returned

Intelligence File

Most newcomers to this concept may frown at the thought of setting up an intelligence file, especially on business associates. The fact is, however, that there are many who wish they had done so long before they got hurt.

This legal size manila folder should contain confidential information about your customer and it should be kept off limits to others. The most common information compiled in this file is:

- **Postal stamped envelopes** - where a discrepancy exists, or is suspected, between the date received and the date claimed in the contents of the envelope.

- **The customer's first transmittal** - where a contractor is invited to bid the job and it lists the drawings he sent. This is strong evidence when the contractor is asked to perform work shown on drawings he didn't know existed.

- **Photocopy of the customer's check** - Suing a deadbeat for money is an inevitable fact of life that sooner or later a contractor will face. Having the customer's banking record handy will greatly facilitate that process. Getting a judgment, at times, is easier than getting a bank account record. Therefore, a contractor should keep an eye on all the checks he receives; they can reveal crucial information about the customer and what he is doing. For example, bank and payer name changes can in some cases reveal a deceptive transition to an entity that has no legal ties with the contractor's contract. Checks that he receives from other parties on behalf of the customer can have a special legal significance. In essence, a contractor should preserve photocopies of all the different bank drafts he receives because once he deposits them their valuable information is no longer in his possession.

- Credit reports- if any.

- **Customer personal data** - Home address, phone, etc.

- **The customer's super**- Home address and phone number, or at least the super's vehicle license plate number and model. The most honorable job superintendent at times gets fired in the middle of the project, leaving behind an array of commitments the customer most often will not honor. When this occurs, this superintendent would welcome the opportunity to defend himself and his commitments out of moral obligation, if only he were asked. However, industry practice and contractual obligations with his former employer prevent him from freely coming forth on the contractor's behalf. Obtaining his address and phone number, should the occasion arise, allows the contractor to get in touch with him promptly, rather than having to track him down through costly and time-consuming legal procedures.

- Auto and truck license plate numbers
- S S # and driver's license numbers
- Occupational and construction license numbers

- **Other subcontractors' data** - Recording other subcontractors' names and phone numbers in this file can help a contractor communicate with those who may experience the same problem he does. Collectively, they may be able to help each other.

Many of these items may seem to be hard to get, but as a contractor sharpens his skills he'll become more vigilant and begin to notice that most of this information, at one time or another, flows right through his office. For example, permit applications, notices of commencement, occupational licenses, and the like, are abundant sources that a contractor can easily access during construction.

FILING NOTICES

Each locality has its own set of rules when it comes to Mechanic's Liens law. If a contractor complies with their rules, and files the appropriate notices in a timely fashion, he will retain valuable rights that will help him protect his investment and collect his money. It is advantageous to learn the local rules and follow their procedures to the letter. In most areas, these procedures can be obtained from the local building and zoning department.

The procedure usually involves the filing of a Notice to Owner and, if a contractor doesn't get paid for his work, of a subsequent Mechanic's Lien within a specified number of days of the commencement and completion date, respectively. In many counties there are specialized private companies performing this service for a nominal fee. This is the best option for most contractors. See Chapter 9, "Collections."

However, no matter who does the legwork, it is imperative that a contractor file all notices on time. The "Notice To Owner" procedure, for those who feel they are offending their customers, is not offensive to those customers that intend to pay; in fact, it's accepted for what it is—a contractor's legal right to protect his interests.

OTHER FORMS OF PREVENTION

Unscrupulous customers, like predators, have a craving for wounded prey. Therefore, anyone who is or appears to be wounded becomes fair game to these predators. That is why the ploy of claiming poverty, used by many contractors, most often backfires and hurts them.

The moral here is that a contractor should not resort to

unnecessary claims when demanding what is rightfully his. In fact, under no circumstances should he ever invoke extraordinary claims. When asking for moneys due him there are two fundamental things a contractor should never say or do: (1) Never explain why he needs the money—the contractor earned the money and it is due him is the best explanation; and (2) he should never say "I'll sue you" or any similar-sounding phrase. A contractor should avoid deadlines—the customer is well aware of the contractor's rights, and the contractor can do as he pleases anytime. Saying "I'll sue you" to some can only be music to their ears.

A contractor telling his customers his financial problems, in the long run, does more harm than good, even when it appears to have been received well. No matter how a contractor looks at it, when he claims hurt to his customers he's a wounded prey. If the customer is unscrupulous, the contractor just walked into his den and, if he's not, this may be the last job the contractor will do with him. Being wounded, or just playing the part, is a losing proposition either way.

Therefore, another good safeguard is to always be financially healthy, if only in the customer's mind's eye. If the customer knows the contractor has the financial strength to wait out the legal procedures, the contractor's chances of collecting are greater than if he claims poverty.

Chapter 9

COLLECTIONS

PREVENTION

One of the most talked about subjects among contractors is how to collect money earned on contracts. The prudent contractors make proper arrangements to collect their money before they extend credit. They also never attempt to collect the full contract amount in a lump-sum payment at the completion of the job. They break down the contract amount in installments, each triggered by a due date. Each installment due date is then set by the completion of certain items of work or a periodic cutoff date. Their contract will also have a specific provision for payment and for work stoppage.

An important thing that will aid the collection of money is the right to stop work when not paid on time. Simply put, a contractor cannot stop working on a job because of late payment and shift the liability to the customer, unless the contract stipulates that the contractor can do so and under what conditions.

Typically, most contractors treat this vital matter lightly and go on signing lopsided contracts subjecting themselves to undue frustrations and to possible losses. An example of a lopsided and uncontrollable provision in a contract is when the contractor agrees to get paid by the general contractor only when the general contractor gets paid by the owner, with no specific due dates set and no rights to stop work.

To prevent unpleasant events, a contractor must read his contracts carefully (see Chapter 6) and ensure that a right-to-stop-work clause is inserted in his contract. The clause need not be complex. In fact, clauses are most effective when handwritten on the contract form at the time the contractor negotiates the contract. Such an insertion may read: *"If the customer fails to make a payment within seven days from its due date, then the contractor has the right to stop work until all moneys due are paid in full."* Then if the customer breaks his promise the contractor can stop work without liability. We should remember that handwritten notes on contract forms take precedence over all other printed matter.

The contractor should negotiate his contract, for no reasonable customer will refuse to negotiate. In fact, many expect a contractor to object and to ask for changes. If he doesn't, the customer may grow suspicious, for they know that most other contractors, rightfully, have asked for the same changes he is asking for now.

PROTECTION

Credit Check

The best protection is knowledge and prevention. A contractor should check all his prospective customers for credit references before he extends credit.

Mechanic's Lien

While a Mechanic's Lien is a powerful legal

instrument, if we don't follow proper procedures and adhere to filing deadlines that lead us to its enforcement, a Mechanic's Lien can be as worthless as a bad check.

The laws that govern Mechanic's Liens vary from state to state. The suggestions that follow are general and presented to acquaint you with the subject. A contractor should learn the specific procedures that are required by the laws that govern Mechanic's Liens in his state and, whenever possible, use the expert services of a lawyer or that of a local filing firm that specializes in this field.

A contractor must make a distinction between Public and Private Properties. Mechanic's Liens are mostly applicable to private properties owned by private owners where the performance of and payment for the work is not guaranteed by Surety Bonds. An owner is a legal entity and can be natural, corporate, or a partnership. Statutory Bonds are not for subcontractors and should not be confused with Surety Bonds.

The Spirit of the Law

The spirit of the law is to protect those who supply labor and material for the improvement of others' properties and prevent the owner from paying twice for the work done. The general concept is for the general contractor to file a notice of commencement and the subcontractors or suppliers to notify the owner that they have been hired by the general contractor to improve his property. Obviously, if the contract is with the owner, the notice to owner is not necessary. Doing so timely, should the occasion arise, gives the contractor the right to file a Mechanic's Lien for money due him on the job and subsequently to foreclose on the property.

FILING

As stated earlier, filing deadlines may vary from state to state; however, taking the State of Florida as an example, the following documents are mandatory, as of this writing, and must be filed within their designated deadlines:

- **Notice to Owner-** must be filed, by a certified service, with the owner and other parties having interest in the property, such as financial institutions, within 45 days from the day a contractor starts work or orders any material or incurs any direct expenses for the job.

- **Mechanic's Liens**- A claim of lien must be filed with the office of the clerk of the circuit court of the county in which the property is located within 90 days from the last time the contractor worked on the job.

- **Lawsuit**- A lawsuit to collect on the Mechanic's Lien must be filed within one year from the Lien's filing date.

RELEASES OF LIEN

Releases of Lien can be conditional and non-conditional, partial or full, each reflecting a specific amount and an effective period-ending date. If a contractor doesn't want to give up his rights to what is rightfully his, he must pay particular attention to the type of instrument he's signing. For example, if he receives a check in payment, he should sign a release that is conditional on the check's clearing the bank.

- **Period-ending-Date**- Regardless of which of the following releases a contractor is signing, each will show an amount and, most significantly, a period-ending date. Of the two, the period-ending date is the most important to consider. It establishes a date beyond which a contractor cannot make additional claims for money due him. In other words, a contractor states that he was paid in full up to and including that date. The amount shown on the release of lien, unless specifically provided for, has no bearing on the release of lien for that period of time. In fact, many releases, even though they are for thousands of dollars, are issued for $10 and other considerations but with a specific period-ending date.

- When a contractor is most concerned with collecting his money, he may inadvertently sign a release showing the amount due him as of the 25th of the previous month with a period-ending the 30th of that month, and at times the 25th or the 30th of another month. In such a case, the contractor has released any work he has done or will do between the 26th of the previous month and the 30th of whatever that month is, even though he was not paid for it.

- When signing releases of lien, always check the period-ending date as well as the amount shown.

- Releases of lien come in many shapes and forms; however, the fundamental thrust of the instrument remains the same. A contractor releases his claim of lien by the amount of money or other compensations he receives for work done on a property. For every partial payment he receives toward a contract he's expected to execute a partial release. When the contractor gets the final payment, then and only then he will execute a waiver or final release of liens.

- There will be times when the customer will expect the contractor to execute a partial release of lien even though he's paying him with a post-dated check. Even though it's a risky business, if a contractor decides to go along with the deal, the least he can do is execute a "conditional release of lien"—the release is valid only if the check clears the bank.

As stated earlier, lien laws, while simple to follow, vary greatly from state to state. The contractor is strongly urged to get acquainted with the laws and procedures of the state in which he intends to work.

Chapter 10

CONCLUSION

All you have read in the preceding pages has been written to stimulate your awareness of the business world around you—the worker who should aim at becoming a Productive Citizen as defined in this book.

I am sure there are many sources out there that can supplement your specific trade or profession's business skills. Nevertheless, there are no others asking individual workers to collectively roll up their sleeves and do what they must to increase their country's productivity level so that in turn they and generations to come can benefit individually from that country's newfound prosperity.

Michael Sammaritano

has written several fiction and non-fiction books.

Keep an eye out for Michael's upcoming works

The Professional Dreamer

Publication Date November, 2011

Published by Adesso Publishing Inc.

Protecting the American Dream

For a complete list of Michael's published and upcoming

books visit

www.adessopublishing.com

Email your comments to

michaelsammaritano@adessopublishing.com

Personal Notes:

Personal Notes:

Personal Notes:

Personal Notes:

Personal Notes:

www.ingramcontent.com/pod-product-compliance
Lightning Source LLC
LaVergne TN
LVHW011352080426
835511LV00005B/244